A Little About Me:

First of all, thank you so much for picking up my book! I hope that this book will give you some insights into becoming happier. But first, allow me to tell you a little bit about myself. I am an extremely happy person. I have a lot to be grateful for including, but not limited to, family, friends, a church home, my dream job, and having good habits for fostering happiness. I truly have it made. But most of my life was nothing like the way it is now. You see, I split my life into three categories: the first 14 years of life, the middle 11, and the last 3. For the first 14 years of my life, I was content but I wouldn't say happy. But I greatly missed that contentment when I turned 14 up until I was just about 25. You see, I have bipolar which is a mental illness that causes depression, and mania, and even made me want to die. Luckily my story had a very happy ending. I am very blessed. But I would still like to explain how this experience affected my happiness then and now.

It was on my 14th birthday that I started showing signs of bipolar disorder. I, nor my family, knew that that was what I was experiencing at the time. It would be over 10 years until I was given the correct diagnosis. Although I didn't realize exactly what I was experiencing, the symptoms still came on really strongly. I suddenly was stressed out about so much and all but completely had lost my ability to feel joy. My depression kicked in and I wished that I was anyone else. This continued on and off for the next 10 years until I was finally put on the right treatment plan. I am sharing this with you because I don't want to give a false impression that I'm just someone who was born happy and has always been that way. If I was then you should definitely not be taking happiness advice from me because I would not know anything about becoming happy.

Luckily, my story of mental illness has a happy ending. When I was 24 I was put on the right treatment plan thanks to many of the amazing people who work for Hartford Healthcare. I now consider myself to be an extremely happy person and look forward to sharing my words of wisdom with anyone who would like to take the time to read this book. I truly hope you enjoy the experience and take away at least one tip from it!

What is Happiness?

Happiness is a term that seems to be defined differently by everyone. Some people think long-term happiness is not attainable because it is impossible to experience positive emotions all of the time. I disagree with this because I do not define being a happy person as feeling great every second of every day. I consider myself to be an extremely happy person but there are plenty of times throughout the day when my mood is neutral and sometimes things do still feel a bit uncomfortable to me. I believe that it's impossible to achieve perfection with any goal; happiness included. But just because we cannot achieve positive emotions every second of every day does not mean that we can not achieve true happiness.

Other people think that it is wrong to focus on happiness because it is a selfish goal. They believe that it is wrong to be happy when so many others are suffering. But happiness is not selfish in the least. I'm sure you've heard of the phrase "misery enjoys company." Well, happiness enjoys company too! The happier we are, the more happiness we can share with others. And what better gift can you give others besides happiness? If you're miserable you will likely take out your misery by harming others and blaming them for it. Back when I was miserable I was very mean to a lot of people who were actually trying to help me. But now that I have happiness I absolutely love sharing my happiness with anyone I can. And making them happier actually makes me even happier!

Another complaint many people have about happiness is that people who are trying to achieve happiness do so by trying to achieve shallow things such as money, material things, or hedonistic pleasures. It is true that many people think that hedonism and material objects will make them happier. And while this can sometimes be true, (I don't know what I would do without my phone or laptop) these things are not what will bring you happiness in the long term and after a while will not bring you happiness even in the short term. What I will be talking about in my book are real things that will allow you to achieve happiness. They're not as simple as material possessions are and will take a lot of work to achieve but if you can achieve them it is almost certain that you will achieve true happiness that will last for years. Possibly even the rest of your life.

But can you train yourself to be happier? Aren't humans wired to be unsatisfied and always looking to gain more things rather than achieving true happiness because of evolution? It is true that our brains, along with the rest of our bodies, have been evolving for millions of years. And it is true that for the vast majority of human history, there was so much scarcity in the world that at least 90% of people lived in extreme poverty thus causing our brains to always be unsatisfied because we needed to look for more. But luckily there is something called neuroplasticity. What this means is that the choices you make and activities you do can literally change the structure of your brain over time. It's not going to happen overnight but by working towards happiness you can indeed change your brain into a happy brain.

I do warn you though that if you expect simply reading this book will make you happier you will be sorely disappointed. So many self-help books promise that if you read them you will become happier because they will give you all of the information that you need. I'm sure if you have tried self-help books before you realize that this rarely pans out. Happiness takes a lot of work. If it didn't, nearly everyone would be happy. And you must realize that there is no one size fits all solution. Working at achieving the things I will talk about in this book will be different for everyone. Humans are unbelievably complex and so is happiness. Some of the advice that you will read in this book may be hard for others but easy for you and vice versa. And there's nothing wrong with that. Our complexity is what makes us human. And it is beautiful. Alright, I think that's enough of an introduction. Let's dive in!

Gratitude: I Know This is a Cliche but Bear With Me

If you've read self-help books or have been to therapy I assume that you have heard about gratitude over and over again. I'm sure it's gotten pretty annoying. You may be pissed at me for starting the book off with such a cliche. I get it but in my defense gratitude really is the first step you need to take in order to be happy. I do believe that it's the most important thing you could do for your happiness levels. So please don't just put this book down. I will try not to just rehash old stuff and instead show you another way of looking at gratitude: changing your mindset.

Many self-help books and therapists will tell you to make a gratitude list of at least 3 things each day. And this is magically supposed to make you feel better. If you're like me you've realized by now that that will not work. But why? Well, it can be summed up by one word: mindset. If you don't truly believe that you have things to be grateful for, writing a list of things that you believe you should be grateful for isn't going to make you grateful. It may even make you feel worse because staring at a blank piece of paper will just make you feel even more like you don't have anything to be grateful for. Lying to yourself by saying you're grateful for certain things doesn't help because you of all people should know when you're lying. So instead of me telling you to just write a list, let me try to explain what I mean in the form of a short story.

Allie is 14 and currently a freshman in high school. She is not a particularly happy person. She doesn't feel that she has much to be grateful for. Her parents are divorced and her siblings are annoying. Her friends are always involved in so much drama. She is an ok student but finds school to be incredibly boring. She also is dealing with all of the pressure these days to get into a top college. Allie is in therapy and her therapist has suggested to she write a gratitude list each week. Allie lists things such as "family, friends, and sushi." Now given she is legitimately grateful for sushi but she gets very little joy out of her family and friends so writing them down on her gratitude list doesn't make her feel any happier.

One day Allie falls ill with a bad fever. It makes her ache all over her body and gives her a throbbing headache. After a week the fever breaks and Allie is surprised to find she now feels happier than she had in a long time. Wanting to discover what was making her happy, Allie decides to analyze the situation. She realizes that when she was sick she kept thinking to herself "things were so great before I got sick. If only the pain would stop." She so badly wanted relief from pain that it caused her to forget about her other problems. Allie decides to try to keep this feeling going. When she has to go back to school and is sitting in her classroom waiting for the class to finally be over she thinks to herself "I'd much rather be in this boring class while being free from pain than at home while in a lot of pain." And when her parents start nagging her about her schoolwork she thinks to herself "they didn't nag me when I was in pain but I prefer nagging to being sick."

Let us analyze the story so far. Allie didn't feel appreciative of her life at first because she didn't see the goodness in the things that she had. But when she lost her health and was in pain she realized that the simple absence of pain is something to be celebrated in itself. This realization can also happen to someone who took food for granted and then ran out of food and learned how much happier they can be if they appreciate the absence of hunger.

Now, this is a little intellectual but bear with me. You may or may not have heard of Maslow's Hierarchy of Needs. It is a popular concept in the field of psychology that looks at what humans need to be happy. It has 5 or 6 levels (depending on who you ask). The first level includes basic needs such as food, water, health, and freedom from pain. Most people in the developed world have most of what they need for this level most of the time. But the problem is when you've had something your entire life it's very hard to appreciate it. It's human nature to always want more so if your basic needs are met you will likely take them for granted. However, if you lose them you will realize, for a little while, how unbelievably essential they are for just getting through the day. But since most people in the developed world usually have these needs met it takes a lot of work to teach ourselves that we should appreciate these things.

One way to increase your gratitude for the basic things is to keep the memory of a time when you didn't have them in mind for as long as you can like Allie did. But this likely won't be enough on its own. It can also be helpful for you to be reminded that many people struggle every day to get the most basic things that you take for granted. Let's start with the most basic: clean water. If you're like me you often neglect drinking water because you prefer better-tasting drinks. Even though tap water is virtually free we still do not want to drink it that often because it's not that exciting. But what if there was no clean water around? And what if you had to spend hours each day working on getting the water that is filled with dirt but that's the best option you have? There are (at the very least) 600 million people who don't have access to clean water and many of them have to walk for miles just to collect dirty water. Now let me be clear, I'm not trying to guilt you into donating. That's not the point of this. The point is to try to imagine what life would be like without clean water. Try reminding yourself that clean water and many other basic needs are not so basic for everyone. Now imagine that you were one of these people and running water was just established in your community. Imagine the relief and happiness you would feel!

It's important to always remember this: the less you need to be happy the happier you'll be. Many of us struggle with thinking that we need more things to be happy. Some things that we want may be good like having friends or doing well in our career. But if we think that we constantly need to add things to our life in order to be happy it will make happiness very hard to achieve. But if we can learn to appreciate what we already have we will make it way easier for ourselves to feel happiness. This is not to say you should never try to achieve anything more than a life with just the most basic needs. Not at all. But appreciating them will not only make you happier but will give you more happiness to invest in getting the other things that you want. (I'll go into more detail on that in a later chapter).

Another basic need that you can train yourself to be grateful for is food. You could practice the same practice we just used for water but I realize different methods will work for different people. Plus it's good to have variety in the approaches you have. What I would suggest for appreciating food is to practice mindful eating. Oftentimes people get so caught up with talking or watching TV while they eat that they don't appreciate how good the food tastes. Instead, we stuff it down and wonder why we're not getting that much joy out of our favorite foods anymore. This can also be a problem if you think about things that are stressing you out while you eat.

So what should you do? Let's say your favorite food is pizza. In my case, it would be pizza with sausage added as a topping. Instead of quickly rushing each bite down our throat let's try to appreciate the wonderful taste. Take a bite very slowly and make sure to chew it slowly. What do you notice? The taste of the cheese? Enjoy the wonderful taste of that exquisite mozzarella. Then taste the tomato sauce. Tomatoes are very popular and for good reason because they have such a delectable taste. Then taste the bread. Enjoy the texture of the bread whether it be a deep dish or thin pizza. Now move on to a piece that has the sausage (or whatever topping you'd like) and notice how well it compliments the taste of the rest of the pizza. Try to do this for each bite. Not only will you enjoy the pizza more but the higher level of satisfaction will fulfill your need for joy with the pizza faster. Therefore, you won't need to eat as much which will save calories and allow you to take some of the pizza home for the next day! All because you truly enjoyed each bite.

I believe I've gone into enough detail about how to be grateful for having your basic needs met. But that on its own will not be enough for you to be truly happy. It will put you in a better mood and thus be able to achieve more happy things, but it's not the only thing I would like to go over in this chapter.

There are so many times in life when things do not go our way and it's hard to be grateful considering the fact that we didn't get what we wanted. Now you've probably heard people say, "just look on the bright side" as if it was that easy. Forcing gratitude is not going to help the situation. You need to address it in a more logical way. You can start by first acknowledging that you have a right to be upset that things didn't go well. It's ok to admit that you're struggling with gratitude. Even if it's just a little thing that didn't go right such as someone giving you a dirty look. And especially if it's a big thing like a breakup with your partner of one year. One thing I constantly want to express during this book is that it's ok not to be happy every second of every day.

Once you've acknowledged your feelings on the situation then you can start trying to see it differently in a logical way. Let's say a stranger gives you a dirty look when you're out taking a walk. Your first response may be to think to yourself "what are they doing giving me a dirty look? I didn't do anything to them! Why are there people like this?" If you stick with this thought process you may begin to have memories of other people being rude to you. This will make you even angrier and will ruin the walk you likely were doing to calm yourself down from the day.

But let's say you take a different route and try to, logically, see what is good about the bad situation. You could ask yourself "does it really matter that this stranger gave me a dirty look?" You may then think "thank goodness this isn't a person who matters to me at all" but if you haven't practiced gratitude a lot you will more likely think "even if it isn't that important it's still a terrible thing for this person to do. Why am I being subjected to this?" And that's ok. If it was easy to turn everything into gratitude, life wouldn't be as challenging as it is.

Alright, so you're still feeling angry. But then you might think to yourself, "is there a reason this person gave me a dirty look?" You may think back to times when you were less than pleasant to others. This likely happened because you were in a crappy mood. But you're not a bad person. You're human. Everyone has crappy moods at least sometimes and unfortunately it may cause us to be rude to others even if they weren't doing us wrong. You may now think "that person's probably in a crappy mood. I'm glad I'm not in a crappy mood. I was feeling good from this nice walk so I shouldn't let this person's misery wash over me." You can also add more grateful thoughts to this. "I'm glad that I worked that out and am able to continue on this nice walk. It was a challenge for me but I overcame it!" A lot of gratitude can come from being grateful for yourself and your own abilities. You can even be grateful for being able to be grateful! Given, this situation isn't the most difficult one to be in but it can still be quite the challenge to change your initial reaction of anger into a reaction of gratitude. If you're able to do it, give yourself a pat on the back!

But why should you try to feel gratitude when doing challenging things? These things are the negative points in your life, not the positive ones. Aren't we only supposed to be grateful for the positive things? Well, so many people don't appreciate the positive things in their lives. In many ways that makes no sense. So finding ways to feel grateful even when times are tough shouldn't be any weirder than that!

But what do you do when you don't want to be grateful? What if things really suck and you need them to change? There are plenty of situations when being grateful would not be a good thing. If you have an abusive partner you shouldn't be saying "I appreciate them so much for making me appreciate the times I'm not getting hit." This sounds obvious but oftentimes people in situations that are horrible and at least seem inescapable will start practicing toxic positivity. I want to make it very clear that toxic positivity is not something I support. Sometimes you do need to realize that a situation is bad and needs to be changed. Especially if it involves you getting abused in some way.

It is important to remember that you need both basic needs and safety needs. Safety needs are the second level of Maslow's Hierarchy of needs. Basic needs and safety needs are so important that you must make sure that they are being met before you try to achieve happiness. Once you have these met they can be wonderful things to appreciate and make yourself happier with. But it would be delusional to try to convince yourself that you can be happy without them. I include this part in this chapter because I do not want anyone to get the wrong idea that I endorse toxic positivity.

Anyway, let's get back to the fun stuff. So this part is about how spirituality has worked for me to become more grateful. This could work for anyone who has any belief in God or multiple gods. And if you don't believe in anything spiritual, which doesn't have to be God by the way, that's ok. There are lots of ways towards gratitude and you have to see what works for you. I am just speaking from my experience.

When I started feeling better because I finally got on the right treatment plan I was, to be honest, very angry with God. I was grateful to not be experiencing mental illness anymore but I didn't understand why God had put me through all that he put me through. I felt like God must've hated me. This feeling stuck with me for quite some time even after I became a happy person. I've heard "God works in mysterious ways" but that was little comfort to me. Mysterious or not, why did God allow me and my family to suffer so much?

As I became happier I began reflecting on my past and on the person I was before I turned 14. I wasn't experiencing mental illness at the time but I wasn't really happy. I was mostly content but that was about it. During my reflections, I realized that if I hadn't dealt with the pain of mental illness I would never have become the happy person that I hope to be for the rest of my life. You see, before I was 14 I believed that happiness was something that happened to you and not something you had to work at. But while I was going through my struggles with bipolar I was working so hard every day just to not feel completely in pain that I learned that good things are worth fighting for and happiness should never be taken for granted. Now let me be clear: I am NOT saying mental illness is a good thing. It was horrible at the time and for so many people it doesn't get any better. But I was blessed that I not only overcame it but actually came out of it stronger than ever before. And God was a big part of that.

As I slowly realized that God didn't hate me I started appreciating my life and God's role in it even more. I was actually already going to church before I made peace with God but now I was going for more than just the sense of community and the wonderful singing. I started believing that God loved me and blessed me in many ways. Yes, my experience with mental illness was horrific and I would never wish it on anyone but perhaps it was true that he worked in mysterious ways.

Soon praising God became a way for me to feel even more gratitude for my life. I started listening to Christian music. I especially liked the songs by Phil Wickham. One of his songs, It's Always Been You, is about how God has always been there during the dark times even when it didn't seem like it. One lyric goes "you are the voice that calms the storm inside me." What this means to me is that God may not magically solve all of your problems but God is there to listen to you and be with you during the tough times even when it doesn't feel like it's enough. Even when I was really feeling alone I now see that God was there for me. He kept me sane enough to get through my battles and come out stronger. And for that I am grateful.

Lastly, I would like to discuss how our culture plays into how grateful people are. I'm referring to American culture but I believe this can be applied to most high-income countries. Now to be clear I am very grateful to live in the U.S. and especially to be living in a first-world country. I'm not trying to insult anyone but I feel like this analysis is necessary for understanding why you may struggle with having gratitude.

Anyway, it may seem like our culture encourages people to be happier because every time you look up "how to be happy" I'm sure you'll find gratitude as one of the top things. But why do we need to be constantly reminded of that? Because our culture does not do a particularly good job of encouraging us to be grateful. We constantly are seeing commercials for material things that we MUST have in order to be happy. Every 6 months there's a new iPhone that comes out and makes the last model seem old and worthless. To be clear, I'm not against people wanting to spend their money on things that could potentially make them happier. What I am critical of is the idea that people NEED the latest phone, purse, or car in order to feel happy. But most people do not realize this.

Thanks to social media people are constantly seeing what their friends are doing and what rich celebrities are doing. We dream of how happy we could be if we could afford a private jet. But many of the rich people who possess these material things really are not very happy. This comes down to a chemical in our brains called dopamine. Dopamine is a chemical that gives us the motivation to achieve things that bring us happiness. It was very useful to our ancestors because they needed to put in so much work just to get enough food to last the winter. But now we live in a world of abundance and there are so many opportunities to experience higher levels of dopamine. This may seem like a good thing at first. Why wouldn't it be good to have more of this happy chemical? The problem is that if the brain is experiencing really high levels of dopamine from one thing for too long it will shut down dopamine receptors thus making it harder for us to get the same amount of joy from the original thing or activity. This is why dopamine plays such a big part in addiction.

Now I'm almost done with this chapter so I apologize if it was boring and/or repetitive to you. I know that gratitude gets talked about in self-help books a lot but I chose to make this first chapter about it because it is so essential as a first step towards being happy. It takes a lot of work to gain happy things, like friends or a career, into your life. But even if you don't have much to start with, gratitude will allow you to get happiness out of those couple of things you do have. And by becoming a happier person you will start to attract more happy things. And then you'll have much more to be grateful for!

Family: Not as Bad as You May Think

Now I do want to make some things about this chapter clear from the start. First of all, I'm not saying that everyone comes from a good family. There are many families out there that are abusive and of course, it is best to get away from these types of families. And I realize that every family has its flaws. I'm not saying that your only chance at happiness is if you come from a good family. Not at all. But if you have a family that makes mistakes but is overall loving this chapter is for you.

When I had bipolar I thought that my parents were evil. You see, in my senior year of college, I achieved my dream of being accepted into several master's programs for social work. I wanted to become a Licensed Clinical Social Worker so I could become a therapist with a private practice. I had decided on this when I was 16 so I was so excited when during that last semester I found out that I had been accepted. But that was really the only good thing about this particular semester. I was experiencing intense depression and mania because my bipolar had gotten out of control. Because of this, my parents did not let me go to graduate school and I ended up having to stay at a residential program for people with mental illness. So yeah…I was pretty pissed.

The real problem though wasn't anyone's fault. I couldn't help that I had bipolar and my parents couldn't help that they were not aware of any good choices. Their original plan was actually for me to stay at home for a year and if I could get myself into a better mental shape I could go to graduate school the next year. But I could not stand the idea of living with them so I started threatening them and they called the police. We definitely had the makings of a dysfunctional family.

The police took me to the hospital and while I was staying there the doctor recommended my parents a place called Blue Sky for me to stay. I was actually happy to go at first because I didn't want to live at home and didn't have any other options for where to live. Soon though I started to really hate Blue Sky which made me all the angrier with my parents. I just couldn't fight the feeling that they hated me and wanted me to suffer. It was a tense situation.

Despite the fact that we clearly were not getting along, my parents continued to take me out to lunch once a week. Sometimes it was ok but many times it led to us fighting. One of the things my parents wanted me to do was to put more effort into my hygiene because I had not been doing that at all during the last semester of college. They had a point. It had actually gotten to the point that I had multiple rashes because I wasn't showering. But I was not seeing things clearly so I didn't put two and two together. The way I saw it was that I was depressed and I didn't enjoy showering so there was no point to it. I'm sure you can understand my parents' frustration.

The reason why I shared this piece of my life with you is that I don't want you to think that I only appreciate family because my family relationships were always easy. It was a real struggle while I was feeling so depressed. And their relationship with me was a real struggle for them too. I was not the most pleasant person at the time, to say the least. I didn't make any sense in my thinking, I wasn't doing the most basic daily tasks, and I was lashing out at them a lot. But now that I am seeing things clearly I realize how lucky I am to have parents that stood by me all of those years that were so difficult and had no promise that things would improve. Within a few months of feeling better, I realized that and am forever grateful. Also, within a few months of me feeling better, my relationship with them completely turned around and we are all now very close.

So many children have difficulties in their relationships with their parents. The interesting thing is that in America and Europe, teenagers hate spending time with their parents while in some other countries, teenagers are happiest with their parents. (I apologize for coming down on our country again. I'm very grateful to live here but I think it's important for us to be able to discuss issues we're having.) This may be because family relationships aren't valued as much here because there is a lot of focus on individualism. And it can be very difficult to deal with one's parents when you're trying to figure out your own way.

And of course, parents do make plenty of mistakes. But this isn't always their fault. For example, for many years parents were told that it is best for their baby to sleep in a separate room and for the parents not to comfort the baby when he, she, or they are crying. Parents were told that giving their babies too much attention would spoil them. Nowadays more professionals believe that it is impossible to spoil a baby and that they need as much loving attention as they can get in order for their brains to develop properly. And I'm sure in 20 years there will be all new theories to raising a child. The bottom line is that sometimes the manual for being a good parent isn't accurate and parents who listen to experts may do their babies wrong.

It's important to realize how hard it is to be a parent. So many times you may try to do right by your kids but you may have been given bad advice. And sometimes there just are no good choices. A parent who wants their child to be more social may end up nagging the kid to make friends so much that the child views making friends as a chore. A parent who wants their child to succeed very badly may start helicopter parenting which will not only annoy the child but will not allow them to figure things out on their own. None of this is meant to excuse parents that are horrible or abusive. It's also not to say that parental mistakes don't do damage to the child. But if you have parents who you know love you it can be helpful to realize that perfect parents don't exist and the fact that they tried their best is worth something.

Parents are not the only part of the family that can help or annoy us. There are also our siblings. In my case that would be a younger sister. For most of my childhood, we had the kind of stereotypical sibling relationship in the sense that we were not big fans of living together. You see, we were very different people back then. My sister was a hard-core extrovert and I was a hard-core introvert. She constantly wanted to play with me but I wasn't having it. And we both had plenty of ways to get on each other's nerves. To make matters worse I was often jealous of her. She always had so many friends and I really struggled in that department. It was a difficult relationship for sure.

Although my sister and I didn't get along so well when we were little things started to turn around a bit when I was 14 and started having problems with mania and depression. My sister was very concerned about me. She would get so upset that I was upset. She would tell me how much she cared about me and wanted to help me. I was shocked to find out that she really cared about me. Our relationship improved but it still needed work.

Years later, when my sister was a freshman in college, I grew closer to her because she was struggling with things I struggled with. You see, despite always making friends so easily throughout her childhood she struggled to find friends during her first semester of college. This really humanized her for me. I had been intimidated by her for so long because I assumed everything that was hard for me was easy for her. But seeing that she struggled made me realize that maybe we could connect over something. And we did. That summer, which was the hardest summer of my life because of bipolar, we spent a good amount of time together. It was literally the only good thing about the summer. And now we are both doing well and talk about once a week. It is nice to have someone about your age who's seen you grow up.

Sibling relationships tend to be difficult for a lot of young people. It makes sense. We didn't choose to be siblings and definitely didn't choose to live together. Some siblings hit it off the bat really quickly which is nice. But for many people, the relationship takes a lot of work. Even though we are being raised in the same house and with the same parents as them, we oftentimes are very different. Even twins oftentimes have very different personalities. This can make it much more difficult to get along. But even if it's not in the cards for you to be friends with your siblings while you're all living together it is important to try to gain a good relationship once you're grown up.

Now of course it is not as simple as just deciding to be friends once you no longer live together. It can be very difficult if you two still are very different people. But there are a lot of benefits to having a good relationship together. You can complain about your parents to each other! And more seriously, you can remember a lot of the same things growing up as kids. And your sibling will always be your sibling unlike friends that you may be close to now but may end up leaving you forever. I'm not saying to plan on being best friends with your siblings but if you can learn to value each other it is very nice to have a lifelong bond with someone who will always be related to you.

Extended family can be very useful too. My grandparents were a big help in getting me through my tough times. I had always been close to them but we became much closer when I started having my issues with mental health. I loved talking to them about things both that had to do with my depression or were just fun to discuss. For a few months in high school, I had a sleepover with them every weekend. They made me feel heard even though my theories on life really didn't make any sense. The good thing was that it wasn't their responsibility to raise me so they didn't have to try to change the way I thought. It was very nice having a nonjudgmental relationship with them.

They were also there for me years later when I was really out of control and going to Blue Sky which I hated. They agreed that it was a bad program. And because they weren't in charge of me they didn't have to just tell me it was the best option there was. They were able to take my side which was such a relief to me. It was nice to have family or anybody that wouldn't try to change me but instead, just listen. I realize that if they were my parents they would've had to do things differently and I'm not saying they were better than my parents. My parents had a very difficult job of trying to get me help when they didn't know what to do and were not given good options. This led to them having to give me tough love which was necessary at the time. But grandparents are luckily there to always be on your side.

Now I realize that many people do not feel the same way about their grandparents. And it's sometimes for good reasons. But what really breaks my heart to see is that people are cutting their grandparents, and other extended family members, out of their lives just because of the family members' political views. I'm not saying you have to agree with everyone in your family. Not at all. You have the right to your opinion. But so do they. Politics is such a stressful topic for so many people these days. I understand that it is very tempting to start fights with people who you think are entirely wrong in their opinions but what does it actually achieve? People aren't going to change their minds if you yell at them for their beliefs. If anything it'll make their beliefs stronger. And whatever happened to agree to disagree? If we could all learn to have calm conversations with people we disagree with, especially family, people would be less extreme and our political choices would probably be better people. But even besides that, there is still a good reason not to let disagreements ruin potentially good relationships with family that will always be there for you.

Music: Not only Wonderful but also Important

Music has always been very important to me. It's helped me with exercise and has been there for me through the rough times too. It seems like everyone loves some type of music. And if they don't they may not have a soul. (I'm joking but also not really.) Listening to music can be such an amazing experience. When the notes being played sound just right and the lyrics mean so much it is pure heaven. Now I'm sure you've had many good experiences with music before but that doesn't mean you're enjoying it as fully as you can. In this chapter, I will talk about different songs that I've listened to throughout my life and what they meant to me. I will begin with songs that I've listened to during my tough times. I highly recommend all of these songs to anyone dealing with a lot or even someone who's just looking for empowering music. I'm not guaranteeing that these songs are for you because different songs work for everyone but I still believe that they can be helpful to most people.

I will start with my interpretation of the song "Shake it Out" by Florence + Machine. The song starts off with the lyrics "Regrets collect like old friends. Here to relive your darkest moments." Back when I was depressed I was constantly thinking about all of the mistakes I had made that led me to the depressed state that I was in. I felt very much that I could relate to this lyric because so much of my life was about living in regret. Even though in reality it wasn't my fault that I had a mental illness I often blamed myself. A little later in the song, it goes "and every demon wants his pound of flesh." This is a reference to a Shakespearian play. I believe what it means in this song is that the bad emotions, which some may see as being the work of the devil, want so badly to hurt you. I constantly felt so much emotional pain from the memories and regrets in my head. I'm very lucky that it never made me hurt myself physically. I'm also very grateful that I heard regrets but not voices like many people with psychosis do. But still, the negative thoughts were so hard to shake off.

The song had gotten off to a sad start but then it begins to get more hopeful by using the lyric "it's always darkest before the dawn." This is my favorite lyric of the song. Of course, I didn't automatically feel better just from hearing it. My depression lasted such a long time that I doubted the dawn would ever come. Still, the song did give some hope. When our lives are very dark and filled with the misery it's nearly impossible to picture things one day getting better. But the beauty of this lyric did bring me some hope. The song goes on to use the lyric "and it's hard to dance with the devil on your back so shake him off." I actually am not entirely certain if I believe in the devil in a spiritual sense but I knew that the song was referring to him in the metaphorical sense. Whether you believe in the devil or not you likely understand how it feels when our entire world is against us and there seem to be evil forces at work. But I hoped while listening to this song, that eventually I would be able to shake off the depression and anxiety. So I now sometimes listen to the song just to remind myself how much better I'm doing and that even if I have a day that sucks, things can get better.

Another song I liked to listen to when I was feeling depressed was "Marching On" by OneRepublic. The song starts out with the lyric: "For those days, we felt like a mistake. Those times when love's what you hate. Somehow we keep marchin' on." There were so many days during my depression when I definitely felt like a mistake. I wished so often that I had never been born. I wished that I wasn't such a burden to everyone. But I liked the encouraging message about continuing to march on. What this meant to me was that life can be a lot to endure and there are going to be very difficult times but if I kept on marching on they may someday get better. At least I hoped.

The song continues with the lyric "for all of the wars we fought." Having depression can be very much like fighting a war. Every day you have to work unbelievably hard just to make it through the day. I was overwhelmed with negative thoughts about how my parents didn't love me, how I had messed up my life by asking for help, and how my future looked so bleak. People who've never dealt with depression may see depressed people as lazy because oftentimes they avoid working and going out. It is often the case that people who haven't dealt with depression think that people with depression just need to cheer up and force themselves to do stuff. They don't understand what it's like to be incapable of feeling joy. Trying to convince them to believe you about how you're feeling can be a battle within itself. That's why this lyric really stood out to me.

The song continues with the lyric "we'll have the days we break and we'll have the scars to prove it." At the time I only wished that I could someday be proud of the emotional scars that signified how I overcame so much. Luckily now I do know that feeling. I often still listen to this song while I'm exercising and it's nice to remind myself that it's ok that my path toward happiness involved a lot of emotional scars because, without my life's ugliness, I would not have the beautiful life I have now.

Another song that I listened to during my depression (this is the last one in this category) was Stand By You by Rachel Platten. The song is about standing by someone you care about. I'm pretty sure it was meant to be a romantic song but music, like any form of art, is up for interpretation. The way I interpreted it was a little unordinary. You see I only have one hero and that is Winston Churchill. Churchill was the prime minister of England during World War II. He knew years before the war that Hitler was evil and would want to take over the world but hardly anyone listened to him. He kept fighting for England to do something about Hitler and they finally did. He played a very large role in defeating Hitler. It could've been a lot worse if Churchill hadn't been around. As a Jew, he is particularly meaningful to me because if Hitler had succeeded in taking over the world I would've never been born. Churchill also had symptoms of depression and some symptoms of bipolar. I find his quotes to be very inspiring and very helpful through tough times. You're probably wondering what the heck this has to do with the song. Well, the way I interpreted it was that Churchill's memory would always be there for me while I struggled to overcome depression.

One of the first lyrics in the song goes "Hands put your empty hands in mine. And scars show me all the scars you hide." While I was depressed I struggled to find someone who I felt really loved me and was ok with my emotional scars. In reality, I had a lot of people who loved me but I was living in my own reality so I felt I had no one. But when I read Churchill's quotes I felt like I didn't have to hide so much. He had often written about the "black dog" which is how he described his depression. He had a lot to deal with, on top of having to defeat Hitler, but he never gave up. In fact, that's one of his quotes "never, never, never give up." As I learned about his battles with depression I felt less ashamed of mine. I believe that by listening to this song you could relate it to God if that's what you'd prefer. I wasn't so certain about God at the time but now I am.

The lyric that keeps getting repeated throughout the song is "Even if we can't find heaven." That's what we should all be looking for: someone to stand by us during the tough times even if it seems the tough times will never end. Now my mental health story did have a happy ending and I am indeed now living a heavenly life. But that doesn't happen for everyone.

Many people deal with years or even decades of life straight from hell. But if you can have someone to go through hell with you it does become a little easier. We should all be so lucky to find that person in our lives or as one of our heroes.

Once I started feeling better (the exact day is December 11, 2019) I started really enjoying music that was about getting through the tough times and coming out stronger. One of these songs was "Dog Days are Over" by Florence + Machine. It was extra interesting because it was made by the same singer that did "Shake it Out." I had moved on from dancing with the devil on my back to dancing so freely. Anyway, the song talks about celebrating being free from the dog days. One lyric goes "the dog days are over. The horses are coming so you better run." I take this to mean that I am now running toward so many good things after being stuck for so long. When I was depressed I was incapable of feeling joy. Depression kept catching me. But once I got on the right treatment plan I was finally able to run towards happiness.

The song continues with the repeated lyric "run fast for your mother, run fast for your father. Run for your children, your sisters, and brothers." I like that the song acknowledges how important family is in finding happiness. My family life has completely changed since I started feeling better. No longer is it all about fighting and feeling like my parents didn't love me. I have built a really strong relationship with them which is actually in part because of the tough times. Although there was a lot of fighting they still stood by me and still loved me even when I was out of control and was so mean to them. I have also become so much closer to my sister in part because she tried to help me during the tough times too. And since I've gotten happier they all have gotten happier too. It's nice that the song acknowledges the importance of the family unit.

Another song that I love listening to in order to remind myself how far I've come is "Good to Be Alive" by Andy Grammar. I love how it not only talks about how awesome the singer's life has become but also what he had to endure in order to get there. One of the first lyrics is "I've been grinding so hard, been trying this shit for years. And I got nothing to show just climbing this rope right here." For so long this is exactly how I felt. I had to try to get better for 10 years before I finally did. And right before I did get better I felt like the 10 years of hard work didn't mean anything because I was still suffering so much. It seemed like there was so much work that needed to be done and I wasn't able to handle any of it.

The song goes on with the lyric "and if there's a man upstairs, he kept sending me rain." I also felt that God was working against me. It seemed like the harder I tried to improve things the worse things got. It seemed like every time I asked for help it just allowed people to hurt me more. I truly did believe that God hated me. But the next lyric is "but I've been sending up prayers and something's changed." I had also been praying without making any progress but then things did finally turn around for me. When I got on the right pills I just knew that it was going to be a new chapter for me. I started to become capable of feeling joy again. It was indeed a miracle.

The song then gets to talking about the fun stuff. It goes "I think I finally found my hallelujah. I've been waiting for this moment all my life." I had been waiting my whole life (or at least the last 10 years) for a moment when I knew everything was going to be ok. And the moment has continuously been improving because of my improved mental health and because of the work I had put into becoming happier. Now my life truly has become one big "hallelujah" and I can't thank God enough for it.

The last song in the category of "reminding me how far I've come" is a song called "For Forever" from the Broadway show/movie "Dear Evan Hansen." In this song, Evan, who has spent his whole life dealing with really bad social anxiety, sings about a perfect day he spent with his best friend, Connor. Now in the story, he wasn't actually friends with Connor but that's beside the point. In this song he sings about the perfect pretend day and how much fun he had and how close he felt to Connor. When I listen to this song I don't think of any person in particular but rather how I used to dream of having such a good day and how I now have good days virtually every day.

The song starts out with the lyric "all we see is sky for forever. We let the world pass by forever. Feels like we could go on forever this way. Two friends on a perfect day." While I was feeling depressed and didn't have any friends for almost a year I often dreamed about how amazing it would be if I could take a break from my problems and go out and have a great day with a friend. I did hope that it would last forever if it happened but I assumed it would never happen in the first place. Now of course the good days have turned into awesome days and they do indeed seem never-ending.

Later in the song, Evan talks about how Connor helped him when he fell from the tree. In the movie, no one helped Evan so he enjoyed imagining that his best friend was there to help. The lyric goes: "I look around and see he's come to get me. He's come to get me. And everything's ok." Everything was ok for Evan in his mind because even though he had a broken arm at least he had a friend who truly cared about him. Back when I was depressed I felt that I had no one because no one cared about me. I am so thankful to have such great friends and family now in my corner. The song is meant to tell the story of Evan imagining that he had a better life but I interpret it as relating to my life as a huge change that was not at all pretend.

As I become happier my gratitude has increased. It makes sense that it would. And since I am a spiritual person it has increased my gratitude to God as well. I now really enjoy listening to Christian music (I'm a Jewish Christian) because it allows me to express my gratitude towards God. If you believe in God these songs could be good for you too. If you don't, that's ok. You just may prefer to skip this section. On the other hand, you may relate it to something else like nature or the universe.

The first song in this category that I will discuss will be "House of the Lord" by Phil Wickham. A few of the first lyrics in the song go "he opened the prison doors. He parted the raging sea. My God, he holds the victory." Before I stopped feeling depressed I felt that I was being imprisoned in a world that was nothing but a nightmare for me. But by the grace of God, I broke away from the depression that was chaining me.

The song goes on to say "we sing to the God who heals. We sing to God who saves." So often we blame God for the bad things that happen in our life but forget to thank God for the good things. We often see bad things as just happening to us, possibly because of God. But when something good happens we often give ourselves all of the credit for working hard to achieve it. Although I do believe that the good things in my life wouldn't have happened without my hard work I also give God the credit for pointing me in the right direction and allowing my efforts to pay off. The song goes on to say "we were the beggars. Now we're royalty. We were the prisoners. Now we're running free." I really do feel that I'm living a royal life now. I'm not rich in the material sense of the world but my life is jam-packed with so many awesome things nearly every day. And being free from depression does indeed make me feel like I'm running free.

Another Christian song I enjoy is also by Phil Wickham. It's called "Falling in Love." The song starts off with the lyric "so much beauty to discover. I can hardly take it." My life now is so filled with such beautiful things and I feel there is so much more to discover. I'm very grateful to God for granting me a loving family, great friends, and an awesome job. But I know there will be more to discover as time goes by. I sometimes get a bit ahead of myself by trying to figure out what God has planned next for me but I realize that it'll be worth the wait. The song goes on with the lyric "we have barely scratched the surface of your death-defying love." God and Jesus have done so much for me because they truly love me. It was hard to feel their love for the longest time but now that I'm doing well and am becoming more spiritual I can feel it. It's amazing how far the love goes. And I'm sure there's far more love to come.

Later in the song, a lyric goes "For the world You made. Every brand new day. For it all, oh God, I say 'I love You.'" There are plenty of times when people, myself included, don't appreciate the little things in life and don't realize how much God must love us to give us so much. Every day is a new journey. A new adventure is to be had. When your days are up you won't get to enjoy all of the wonderful things about our world. Or enjoy what God has planned. Of course, there are plenty of negative things going on whether it be on the news or in our own lives. It can be very tempting to get upset and be ungrateful towards God when bad things happen. I struggle with this myself at times. But I try to remind myself that even if things aren't perfect they are a million times better than they used to be. God's plans for me may be complicated and mysterious but they can also be beautiful if I make sure to see it that way.

The last song I will provide an analysis for is the song "We Praise You" by Brandon Lake. I only heard this song a few weeks ago but it's a lot of fun to watch especially if you watch the concert version. It starts out with the lyric "let praise be a weapon that silences the enemy. Let praise be a weapon that conquers all anxiety." I have a lot of praise for God because of how awesome he has made my life. I admit I do sometimes still fall back into feeling ungrateful at times. But when I stop to think of how great God is and how great he has been to me it automatically lifts my spirits. It is so important to praise God every day because it is such a powerful form of gratitude. When we praise him our other problems seem to just melt away and everything becomes better.

The line that will be continuously repeated throughout the song is "this is what living looks like. This is what freedom feels like. This is what heaven sounds like." I'm not saying that believing in God will necessarily make you happier and living without God will make you unhappy. But in my experience, it has been so freeing. I feel like I can see the world's beauty so much more because I know that it is all part of God's plan. And I enjoy it so much more because praising God allows me to experience more gratitude for my life. I'm not saying that this is how it works for everyone but it has worked so well for me.

One of the biggest privileges of modern technology is that it allows us to listen to music whenever we want. It used to be that only the richest of the rich could afford orchestras or go to the opera to hear music. And even then they were very limited in what songs they could listen to. But now everyone has access to millions (if not more) of songs. And it is so cheap. We need to appreciate the wonders of what it's like to have music right at our fingertips. Given, the average American does listen to quite a bit of music. But I believe we should be replacing watching TV with listening to even more music because music is literally food for your soul while TV can be stressful at worst and a waste of time at best. I will discuss this more in my chapter about avoiding bad-happiness investments. I hope that you find the right kind of music for you that can help you get through the most difficult of times.

Using the Hard Times to Your Advantage: More than Just Looking on the Bright Side

Allow me to begin with a question. What does the Black Death have to do with the Renaissance? For those of you who are unaware, the Black Death (or Black Plague) was a disease that spread around Europe at the end of the Middle Ages. It killed off one-third of Europe's entire population in just a matter of years. I think we can all agree it was a very bad thing that happened. But what about the Renaissance? The Renaissance was the period right after the Middle Ages when Europe flourished. You may have heard about the wonderful art that was created during but it was more than that. So many new inventions were created. Wages in Europe also started to go up which hadn't happened in hundreds of years. So why did the Renaissance all of the sudden happen after the Middle Ages? Because of the Black Death.

You see, before the Black Death, there were many peasants around to do the work of very few rich people. The rich people paid them wages that kept at least 90% of the population in a state of extreme poverty. But after the Black Death, there weren't as many workers so they started to negotiate better salaries because their labor was more valuable than during the Middle Ages. Given, it still took hundreds of years to pull people out of extreme poverty but it was a start. And rich people started investing more in inventors and artists which slowly increased the amount of wealth in the world.

So why am I giving you a really boring history lesson in a book that's supposed to be about happiness? It's because if you look throughout history you can see that many horrible things actually have led to many good things. Now, this is not to say that the Black Death was a good thing or that it didn't lead to suffering. It just means that humans sometimes thrive under difficult conditions. We really can't tell how things are going to turn out until so many years later. I'm sure no one thought the Black Death was going to actually improve the lives of Europeans at the time. But you never really know exactly how things are going to turn out so it's best to do your best to use these bad times to your advantage.

Since I am a Jewish Christian I have been very interested in two events that happened during the first century. I'm sure you can guess the first one. You got it: Jesus suffering and dying for our sins. What I find most interesting about it is not that Jesus just suffered at his death but he knew how his life was going to end the whole time. He could have chosen a different path entirely that wouldn't have led the Romans to crucify him. But he knew that would be cheating humanity out of why he was brought into the world. He needed to preach about loving one another and realizing that God loved us even though it led to the Romans crucifying him. He loved us and thus was willing to sacrifice for us.

The next event that happened in the first century that inspires me is likely not one that you've heard about. You see, Jews, on average, tend to be very educated and successful in many fields. But why? Well, it's actually because of their enemy: the Romans. What happened was that around 70 A.D. the Romans fought the Jews because the Jews were rebelling under Roman law. The Romans killed off many of the Jewish leaders. This led to the rabbis having to become the leaders of the Jewish people. The rabbis were the ones that studied the Torah and needed to be well-educated. But now that they were in charge they decided that all Jews rich or poor should be educated. (Yes this didn't technically include everyone because it didn't include the women but it was 2,000 years ago so have some perspective.) Anyway, this led to all Jewish boys being required to go to school from age 6 to 13. Then they would have their Bar Mitzvahs. And although it wasn't required it was encouraged for teenage boys to continue their studies after their Bar Mitzvahs too. What effect did this have? Well, in 70 A.D. over 90% of Jews were farmers. 100 years later almost 90% of them were in jobs that required reading and math skills. This is not to say that Romans were good people who were trying to help Jesus and the rest of the Jews. Definitely not. But just because someone or some force out there that has been trying to defeat you seems to have won does not mean that's going to be the end of your story.

I would now like to tell you more about my journey toward happiness. It started on December 11, 2019. I had been dealing with depression and mania for a long time but then I was finally put on the correct medication. I'm not saying that medication is always the answer to mental illness but for me, it finally worked. It was not without a lot of waiting and hardship though. I started showing signs of mental illness when I was 14 so my parents had me start therapy. A year later it still didn't seem to be working so they had me meet with a psychiatrist. After that, it was 9 years of being on pills, being off pills, being back on pills, stopping the pills without permission, and just nonstop back and forth.

Those 10 years I was struggling with were quite awful, to say the least. I would never wish it on anyone but I am glad that I went through the experience because it made me the person I am today. Now to be clear I am NOT SAYING THAT MENTAL ILLNESS IS A GOOD THING. Not only is it a horrible thing to go through but many people never get better from it. And I'm not saying that I just had to "look on the bright side" and boom I was cured. Absolutely not. I needed help because I had a medical condition and it took a long time for me to get the right help. But thanks to my experiences of just trying to get through each day I learned not to take happiness for granted.

You see, before I was 14 I thought that happiness was something that happened to you. I thought I would be happy once I had a boyfriend, then a husband, then a couple of babies. So many people fall into this trap of thinking they'll be happy once they get what they want. I'm sure you've heard of "money doesn't buy happiness" but I'm not just referring to material things. Even if you're aiming for the things that society tells us to aim for (such as a prestigious job, a spouse, or kids) it's not accurate to think that you'll be happy once you gain those things. True happiness comes from within. That's why the first chapter of this book is about gratitude.

Anyway, let's get back to December 11, 2019. I wasn't happy automatically. I was very excited for one day that it seemed like I was on the right pills but then I slipped back into being unhappy. I realized that the pills were working to make my mania and depression asymptomatic but they would not be enough for me to become happy on their own. But the one thing I now had was gratitude that I finally had my mental health back. It helped me gain perspective on my days. Instead of being upset that things still weren't going well, I focused on my gratitude. And over time things improved.

Now I at least don't mean to say the classic line: "everything happens for a reason." There are many truly awful things that can happen to you and while they are happening it would actually be a sign of mania if you were happy through them. And I am not saying that if you don't get over the stress of your past in 2 seconds there's something wrong with you. It's natural to feel negative emotions after something bad happens to you. Denying this will lead you to push down your feelings and make yourself feel worse. All I am saying is that just because something bad or even truly awful happens to you it doesn't mean that you're doomed to a life of misery. You may never feel like this bad thing happened for a reason but you can use it in many ways to not over overcome the challenge but become stronger because of it.

I'm sure, for many of you reading this, that this is a very uncomfortable topic. I'm sure some of you have been through really difficult times and don't want to hear that it was a good thing that they happened. Many of you may feel that if you use your experiences as a way to make yourself happier it's letting the people who did terrible things to you win. Because if what happened to you turned out to be a good thing then wouldn't it make those who have harmed you seem like good people? This is definitely something that doesn't have an easy answer. What I think is best to focus on though is not whether or not those who hurt you were bad people but how you can stop punishing yourself for what they have done. It's not for them, it's for you. Just because people tried very hard to hurt you permanently does not mean that they have to succeed. And I know that's much easier said than done. But when you put in the hard work to do this you need to know that you're doing it for yourself and not anyone or anything that caused you pain.

I would also like to add that I want you to think about adding this way of thinking to your own life but I DO NOT want you to force it on others. Telling someone who's experiencing trauma or sickness to "just get over it" is not at all helpful. It's a very difficult thing to do and everyone's journey toward healing is their own, not something others can force on them. If you make them feel that they need to hurry up and get over it, you're telling them that their feelings don't matter and they should just stop being a burden to everyone else. This will really mess up their healing journey quite a bit. They need to heal for themselves not please anyone else. And it is not your place to rush them. Focus on healing from your own pain, not on forcing others to hurry up the process of healing from theirs.

The World: Time for Some Negativity

Most people assume that if you're happy you'll be optimistic about the world and if you're depressed you'll be pessimistic about it. But in my case, it was the opposite. Back when I was depressed I needed something to be positive about. I needed that so badly. So I would learn facts about the worst things in the world and put a positive spin on them. Oh, 5 million kids die every year before turning 5? Well, that's great because it's much less than it used to be. There's war and genocide going on? Well, that's ok because the world has lowered violence. I was practicing what I hate so much: toxic positivity. I did this because I was so depressed about my own life that I needed the world to seem at least somewhat positive. But over the last few years, I've not only gotten happier but also have seen the world in a more realistic way which tends to be pessimistic. Go figure!

Now you may be wondering "why would someone writing a book to teach about happiness mention the negative things in life?" Well, it's because I don't want you or anyone reading this to get the false idea that I'm seeing everything in the world through rose-tinted glasses. I'm not someone who goes around telling everyone "oh the world is so wonderful. You just have to look and you'll see the positive." There are many wonderful things about our world. I've been blessed with many of them. But there's A LOT of messed up stuff in the world too. I mean just watch the news. So many awful things. And there's so many awful things that are changing society on a daily basis that don't get talked about nearly as much as they should.

Even if you aren't living a horrible life of being severely ill or abused there are still plenty of bad things out there. Schools are teaching kids useless information and not preparing them for the real world, so many people don't like their jobs, and politicians manage to somehow get even more corrupt each day. Just to name the most obvious ones. If it were up to me things would be different. I would make Montessori education (which involves kids learning things they're actually interested in) the norm. This would lead to many more people knowing what field would make them happy to work because they were able to pursue their interests as kids. I believe that would help things a lot. But that of course would not fix all of the problems. And, more importantly, it's not up to me.

So many people dream about being a hero and fixing all of the world's problems. I was this type of person for years. Back in high school, college, and even after college, I thought I would be the driving force behind ending poverty in the world. Why I thought that when I had only taken one economics course in college, and didn't even do well in it, I don't know. In part, it was because I wanted to help people. And in part, it was to feed my own ego. I kept planning that someday I would have billions of dollars to donate by convincing people worth billions of dollars to not only donate the money but leave it up to me to decide where it would best be donated to. I was in no way qualified for that position but in my mind, I would've been perfect at it. In the end, that of course never happened.

It's very common for teenagers and especially college kids to want to save the world. This could be done by addressing so many different issues whether it be ending world hunger, destroying corrupt governments, or reversing climate change. I'm not saying that these issues don't matter but the fact is they're not going to be solved by average people. The problems may be partially fixed by genius scientists or people in positions of power. But they're not going to be solved by a couple of college kids marching on the streets with unbelievably oversimplified understandings of the issues. Sorry for being negative. (Not really though.)

It sucks that there are so many problems in the world. And it's ok to acknowledge that. You can still be happy without the toxic positivity of believing that everything in the world is going great when it's clearly not. But how can I be extremely happy and feel so negatively about the world at the same time? Well, it's because of where I put my attention. There are literally billions (if not trillions) of things going on every day in the world. We can't possibly notice them all. So what we as humans do is decide where to put our attention. I used to put a lot of my attention into politics and global issues. I thought that this would help me solve these issues.

But I've yet to influence politics or global issues at all. I don't need to know about all of those things because I'm clearly not in a position to save the world. But I am in the position to save my own life from turning into a miserable existence.

It may sound selfish to know about the endless amount of problems in the world and not worry about them. But if you actually think about it logically you'll realize that you become negative because the news not only does not help the world but actually harms it. If you're in a bad mood you'll likely be mean to others. Especially if they don't agree with you about how you would go about saving the world. So many people these days cut off their own family members just because they have different views about the world. Now obviously if you have a family member who's doing things to harm you or others it makes sense to protect yourself from them. But just having a different view from yours on its own doesn't mean that's necessary. But if you spend hours each day watching and/or reading about the news you will become so obsessed with it that it will become an identity to you. This is not a good strategy for saving the world because it will only further divide us all.

Anyway, the reason why I wanted to include this part in my book is that I want to make it clear that being a happy person doesn't mean thinking everything is wonderful. So many people hate the idea of being happy because they view it as delusional. But it's not delusional to say "yes there are a ton of problems in the world but I don't have the power to fix them so I'm going to make the world a better place by creating more happiness for myself and those that I care about." If more people did this people on both sides of the political spectrum could calm down and stop being so vicious to one another. And that would make the world a better place.

Exercise: I Hear you groaning but Hear me out

Americans are constantly being told that they need to exercise in order to achieve a healthy weight. There are now so many gyms that millions of Americans have joined. That's not to mention all of the at-home workout products that are being sold. And yet very few Americans are getting enough exercise. But why? Well, it likely is due to the fact that most Americans exercise solely for what it can do for their bodies. Want to drop 20 pounds? Exercise. Want to become extremely muscular and have a 6 pack? Exercise. Want to feel happier? What does exercise have to do with that? We have been so focused on what exercise can do for our bodies that we forget the body part exercise has the biggest impact on: the brain.

I was never really into the gym but my dad used to be into it. The reason why he switched to exercising at home is because of how annoyed he would get with the gym during the months of January and February. You see, so many people make New Year's resolutions to lose weight. They join the gym in January with lots of motivation to work out so hard that they'll burn that excess belly fat. For a couple of weeks, the gym will be packed with people like this. And then they'll lose interest and not come back anymore. This is why gyms usually require a one-year membership fee instead of month-to-month because they know most customers won't be there for long. But what's causing them to lose motivation towards exercising? The answer to this is actually pretty simple. Humans don't have the energy to stay excited about a goal for that long. So if they don't enjoy exercising eventually their will power will die and they'll lose motivation to push through. There's got to be a better way. And there is: to enjoy it.

But isn't exercise supposed to suck? Isn't it supposed to be painful? What about the philosophy of "no pain no gain?" Well, that's just it. People see exercise as something that sucks. And to be fair the way they do it usually sucks which reinforces their belief. They set impossibly high weight loss goals for themselves and then just suck it up until they lose the motivation and can't stand to make themselves miserable any longer. But the reason why people hate to exercise is not that it's a horrible thing. It's because we make it into a horrible thing by having the assumption it's going to suck. If we could see that exercise is meant to be enjoyed we would put more work into finding a version of the exercise that is enjoyable to us.

Take me for example. I hate running. I hate jogging. But I love walking. Back when I was in school and we had to run a mile in under 11 minutes I tried hard and was in so much pain and still did not pass. I have running asthma so as soon as I start running, jogging, or going uphill I really feel like I can't breathe. I hated when we had to exercise in gym class by running laps. And yet I would often take short walks in order to help myself think. Walking is something most people do every day so our bodies are meant for it. And there are people out there who love running and I'm not at all against that. It just doesn't work for me. What I enjoy doing is either walking or doing step aerobics. And that works for me.

But why would walking for exercise feel good? Well, I'm not that good at science but here's a very simplified answer: it releases endorphins. Our bodies want to encourage walking a lot because we evolved as hunter-gatherers and had to walk long distances to find food. Walking for a long time can be tiring or even painful so our body manages that by releasing endorphins. Endorphins are a feel-good chemical that not only suppresses the pain but can literally give us a natural high. Another reason exercise feels good is that we breathe faster so we take in more oxygen which is also great for the brain. But if we're struggling to breathe because we're doing exercise that is too intense we're not going to feel good.

I have loved exercise for a long time. Back in high school and college, I would do step aerobics while watching a movie or some music videos on my laptop. Eventually, I switched to walking. I now walk 2 hours a day almost every day. Not only is it helping me lose weight but I will continue doing it for the rest of my life (assuming I'm able to) because it is so good for my mental health. It's a great opportunity for me to listen to music and even sing along while I'm walking. It is very helpful in relieving stress and just making the day even better. Unfortunately, this is not how it is for most.

So many people who exercise do it solely to lose weight. They choose an activity that's really high intensity and even painful because their bodies are not ready for it yet. They insist on things like "willpower" and "push yourself" because they are in such a rush to lose weight and never have to exercise again. Of course, even if they do lose the weight if they stop exercising they're just going to gain it back. This is why at least 90% of people gain the weight they lost during a diet back within 2 years. And then they start the same process over again of torturing themselves until they lose the weight again and again.

When you are choosing the type of exercise you want to do it's best not to be in a rush. It can take time to find the right type of exercise and the right intensity. If you haven't taken long walks in years you're not going to be able to start out with 2 hours a day. So instead start out small but focus on making it as fun as possible. If you take 15 minutes a day to walk and really enjoy the scenery of nature and/or the sound of music that you're listening to you'll naturally want to do more. It took me almost 2 years to get into the habit of walking 2 hours a day. If I was in a rush to lose weight that would've really bothered me. But I knew that exercise could be a lot of fun so I worked hard at it. And because it was enjoyable it didn't feel like hard work at all. And that's what exercise is meant to be: a fun way to lower stress, get healthier, and yes lose weight.

Why Everyone's Trying to Escape Reality

I'm sure you've heard people say that we all should be grateful that the world has gotten so much better. They say that life is so much easier now, at least in the developed world. But then why are depression and anxiety on the rise? By so many objective measures life in most of the world has improved. We have vaccines and antibiotics so we don't have half of our kids dying before the age of 5. America produces way more food than we need so starvation is rarely an issue. Not to mention the fact that more people than ever are literate and going to college. So why all of the anxiety and depression?

Before I tell you my theory on this I want to make it clear that I have had dozens of theories to explain this and I'm sure I'll continue to come up with new ones. You don't have to take my theory that seriously it's just something to think about. Ok now that that's out of the way, my latest theory is that the world changing so quickly, even for the better, causes us humans to not know how to handle life.

First, let's look at history. Humans have been on Earth and have been evolving for millions of years. (You may believe it's been thousands and that's fine my point is just we've been around for a long time.) Like all animals evolved under natural selection humans evolved in order to survive in their environment. It was a tough environment to survive in. It was filled with animals who wanted to eat us and oftentimes did, diseases that we couldn't protect ourselves from, and mass famines. Not the greatest environment to live in. And things changed very slowly. It was only about 13,000 years ago that humans started farming. And that led to higher population growth which made it easier for diseases to spread. The main point I'm trying to make is that although life was quite terrible, humans managed to carry on.

Then about 250 years ago the Industrial Revolution took off. This led to new inventions and new business practices. Many people will argue that this was not a good thing because of greed and CO_2 being released but it did have one upside to it: huge decreases in poverty. Back in 1800, it was estimated that about 90% of humans on Earth were living in extreme poverty (less than 2 dollars a day). Today 10% of humans are. So there's still work to do for sure and I realize just making $2 a day is not the end goal but you got to admit that's pretty impressive. But 250 years is such a short time from an evolutionary perspective so our brains have not had time to evolve to this new world.

Let's look at food as an example. It used to be that humans viewed food unanimously as a good thing. It made it so that farmers would work crazy long hours in order to make sure that they could grow enough to feed their families. And so often, especially during the winter, humans wouldn't have enough food and were at risk of starving to death so they dreamed of a world where food was cheap and plentiful. Now that dream has come true for most people and it's not going so well. Because there's so much food EVERYWHERE and so much of it is full of the fat, sugar, and salt that we love, food has now begun to be seen as a problem. Americans are constantly dieting and turning down food that they could eat because they're so concerned about their weight. And for good reason because eating too much food (especially with fat, sugar, and salt) can lead to diabetes, heart disease, and probably cancer. We don't know what to make of this. How could something that people used to love so much and work so hard for become something that's destroying us? Our brains evolved to tell us to eat as much as possible because food used to be so scarce. It has no idea what to do about food when it is so abundant so our once pure loving relationship with food has become a nightmare.

I'm sure you've probably heard about dopamine in the news. In case you haven't, dopamine is a chemical in our brains that rewards us for doing something productive and helps us stay motivated to keep getting it. Not that long ago this was a very good thing. It took so much work to survive so dopamine helped us work hard to get food and everything else we needed. But now there's something that provides us so easily all of the dopamine we'd want and then some: social media. Getting likes on Facebook or getting retweeted on Twitter has been shown to increase dopamine in our brains. And it's so easy to get. But that's where it gets complicated. You see if your brain is experiencing too much dopamine it will decrease the number of dopamine receptors thus making us require more dopamine to get the same good feeling. This is why doing the same enjoyable thing over and over isn't as much fun as it was in the beginning. And that's where addiction starts. When you want that dopamine rush so badly that you use social media for hours each day and freak out when you're not getting liked or retweeted. It will also make you less likely to be able to enjoy doing good stuff that could give you a little bit of dopamine like going to work. Dopamine, which used to be so useful in helping us obtain what we needed, has now become a dirty word.

Family structure has also greatly changed. It used to be that everyone who had kids was doing so as a retirement plan. Parents would take care of children and teach them how to run the farm so the kids would take care of them when they were old. Thus the family structure needed to be strong or else they wouldn't have been able to work together in order to just barely survive. But having a close family structure came with other benefits than just survival. Yes, there were bad families that made people miserable but most of the time having the whole family living and working together created strong bonds between the parents and children. This is still true in many parts of the world. Latin America especially is full of countries with strong family ties. And in a study that asked people if they had had at least 5 positive experiences the day before, most of the top 10 countries were in Latin America. Family can bring a lot of joy. But it takes work.

Nowadays, in many developed countries, family isn't seen as being as important as it used to be seen. People are wealthy enough to afford to live on their own without depending on their family's help. Now I'm not saying that financial freedom is a bad thing but it has changed the way people view family. At the time of my writing this book, it's almost Thanksgiving. It's one of the few occasions where families see more distant relatives. And it is so stressful. People are perfectly fine starting fights with their family members over politics. The thinking used to be don't discuss politics but nowadays that's the main thing people are discussing. If people were dependent on their families they would likely put in the effort to at least get along for one meal. But people are putting their own egos first and shattering relationships with aunts, uncles, grandparents, and even parents in order to feel like they spoke their minds. And so people are feeling much less joy these days from their families.

Now, none of this is to say that it's all society's fault if we're unhappy. I believe it is important to take personal responsibility but I don't think it's a bad thing to acknowledge the fact that this new reality is exhausting our brains. And it seems to be getting worse because now we are doing so many harmful things to escape reality. Drug use is up and virtual reality experiences are becoming more common. People are trying to get more dopamine in an artificial way which is just going to lead them to need more and more.

Luckily there is a way to be happy with all of these things going on. We can train our brains to better adapt to this new type of world. We can try to be grateful for and work at things such as family relationships. We can cut down on social media (I recently started doing that and it's really not as hard as I would've predicted.) We can try to be grateful for having healthy food available for us to eat. None of this is easy, especially because our brains are going to require a lot of work to change. But if we were living in the old world we would have to be spending that energy on trying to not starve to death. Now we can focus our efforts on not doing things to death. And we can be grateful to have the opportunity to become the happiest humans have ever been!

Helping Others: Be a Helper Not a Hero-Wannabe

You might be a little confused as to what I mean by a hero-wannabe. Allow me to explain. There are two main paths you can take when it comes to your strategy for helping others. The first is the hero-wannabe path. Now there have been people throughout history who were legitimately heroes but these people were mainly brilliant scientists, people in power who risked everything to stand up to evil, and people who risked or even gave their lives to save others. They without a doubt make up less than 1% of our population. But there are plenty of hero-wannabes out there who think they are meant to be heroes when they're clearly not. Then there are helpers. Helpers do things to help others that can be big or small. But they don't force themselves onto people who don't want or are not ready to be helped. However,-hero wannabes oftentimes include themselves in situations that they are not equipped to handle and oftentimes make things worse.

Let's look at the example of blood transfusions. Blood transfusions were made possible by a handful of biologists. They are all heroes and should be given much applause for allowing over 1 billion lives to be saved. But although there were only a few heroes when it comes to blood transfusions there have been millions and millions of helpers: people who donate blood. Blood transfusions being invented and made safe would be useless if everyone stopped donating blood. Now I don't believe that simply having some blood drawn makes you a hero but it does make you one of the so many helpers that have allowed over a billion lives to be saved.

But what's wrong with trying to be a hero? If you're meant to be a hero that's one thing but very few people are. Hero-wannabes manage to make themselves feel good while harming so many people. Hero-wannabes oftentimes are young people who want to make the world a better place but have no actual knowledge of how to do so. Imagine if someone who was a high school student tried to do surgery on people who couldn't afford surgery. These high school students may convince themselves they're being a hero but in reality, they're just killing people off. So why should it be any different for people with no knowledge about the world to change the world in any way?

If you are a caring person you're probably thinking now how you can become a helper. Well, it's unfortunately not always easy. Take me for example. I am now working at a clinic that provides care to people experiencing mental illness. I am a recovery support specialist there who is someone who's dealt with mental illness in the past, is now in recovery, and helps people who are currently experiencing mental illness. It's provided me with many opportunities to help others and I absolutely love it. But it is hardly the beginning of my journey of searching for ways to help others.

I began volunteering when I was 12 as a part of my Bat Mitzvah requirement. I volunteered at Jewish Family Services where I provided child care for a few hours so foster parents could meet and discuss their experiences. It was a lot of fun and I felt good being a help. But it was only once a month and I wanted to do more. After that, I tried to find more ways to help. But it was hard. I did some work at the Jewish Family Services food pantry but it wasn't interesting at all and I didn't feel fulfilled. I tried finding other volunteer opportunities but they were hard to come by if you were a 12-year-old. When I was 16 I was able to start volunteering for Habitat for Humanity. They do a lot of good work that helps people get better living conditions but all I would ever do was paint which was boring to do for 6 straight hours so I still didn't feel fulfilled. I was certain though that once I started college I would find something better.

During the first semester of college, I took a class that required volunteer hours. They had four choices of where to volunteer and I chose to volunteer at the Boys and Girls Club. I do believe that it's a good organization for providing structure and a free dinner to kids but I did not particularly enjoy volunteering there. The problem was the kids were a little older so they weren't interested in playing with me so I ended up just being on my phone a lot. But then near the end of my freshman year, I started volunteering for Horizons for Homeless Children. I would go to a homeless shelter once a week and play with kids for 2 hours. It could be fun because I love little kids but some of the kids were quite difficult. And some of the parents acted pretty badly around the kids. It was tough. When I finished college I had a difficult time finding a job and I couldn't do Horizons for Homeless Children anymore because I was in a different state. So I volunteered at a historical museum. It was so unbelievably boring.

The years went by and eventually, I recovered from bipolar so I took a class to become a Recovery Support Specialist. After I passed the class the teacher got me a paid internship as a Recovery Support Specialist at Trinity College. It was fun and I did feel like I was helping. But the internship was only meant to last 12 weeks. Afterward, it took me over a year to find another job as a Recovery Support Specialist. But I finally have and I am loving it. After 15 years I finally found the fulfillment of helping others that I always wanted.

The reason why I shared this long story with you is that I want to make it clear that I realize getting an opportunity to help others is not as easy as people think. So many people think that if they just make the choice to dedicate their time to others they'll find fulfillment easily.

But this is rarely the case. You can volunteer but it is very difficult to get a volunteer position where you're really making a difference because organizations do not want to give volunteers much responsibility. And finding a job that helps people can also be difficult. If I had the exact same job but the staff members were all very mean I would hate it and would likely not be able to help people. Helping others is a privilege that we should all try to obtain but also must realize is not easy to come by.

You are likely thinking to yourself "if the chapter is about helping others in order to become happier, why is the author just telling us how hard it is to find opportunities to help others?" Well, the ways I've been discussing a way to help others are organized work and volunteering. But just because good work or volunteer positions are hard to come by does not mean that it's impossible for people to find ways to help. This is going to sound cheesy but you can always find ways to be a helper by just helping the people in your own life. It can be as simple as telling your parents you love and appreciate them or listening to a friend vent. I know this doesn't seem like much but if everyone put in the effort to be nicer to everyone else the world would change so dramatically. You're not going to become a hero by doing it but that's ok. You can be part of a group of billions of helpers. And that counts for something and successfully making those you help happier will bring you more joy too!

The Joy of Learning: Don't Let School Ruin this for You

So many people falsely believe that learning is supposed to be a stressful thing. We learn this in school because we are constantly having to memorize information for a test and are told we are failing if we can't memorize information fast enough. But learning is so much more than just the useless information we get at school. Now, to be fair, I actually enjoyed school because I was good at memorizing useless information and to this day I keep educating myself on mostly useless facts. But over time I'm discovering ways to think more deeply about life and learning has helped me change my perspective on so many different subjects.

So many kids hate school but that isn't because they don't love learning. They are born to love learning because that's what they do nearly every second of every day when they're babies. The whole world is new to babies. They're born not being able to talk or even understand who Mommy and Daddy are. That's why they sleep so much because that much learning can be exhausting. But over time they start to catch on to the way things work. The first 5 years are so important because by the end of the 5th year, the child's brain is 90% developed. But just because they have only 10% of their brain left to develop does not mean that learning is not still important. We just have to give them the opportunity to learn things that actually interest them instead of boring them to death.

But why is school teaching such useless information? Well, it goes back to the idea of the world is too full of abundance for us to handle. Back not that long ago it was assumed that if you were born to a farming family, as most people were, you would become a farmer. That was supposed to be your only career option. So you would grow up doing chores on the farm and learning how to someday run it. The education was full of useful information because your parents would only teach you what you needed to know to run the farm and farming used the exact same techniques for most of human history. But now it is no longer assumed you will follow in your parent's footsteps. There are thousands (if not more) of types of jobs out there. This could be a very good thing since if you have so many choices there's bound to be one that fits your interests and skill sets. The problem is that schools cannot possibly train you for thousands of types of jobs. So school has become not a place that will prepare you for a career but an institution to prepare you to sound smart at dinner parties when topics such as literature and history come up.

But what should kids learn in school? Well, if I had a ton of money and was super powerful (which may happen someday) I would want to greatly increase the number of Montessori schools in America. Montessori schools allow children to learn through play and pursue their own interests. Children are able to learn what interests them and what they're skilled at thus making childhood so much more fun and finding the right career much more likely. And studies have shown that adults who attended Montessori schools as children are happier. I'm sure kids would love it and parents would learn to love it after seeing how much it makes their children love learning. Unfortunately, I'm not (yet) rich and powerful so I'm not going to be opening up any schools any time soon.

You may be wondering why I'm telling you about the problems and solutions of our public school system when you are (I assume) an adult who doesn't see the point of learning more because you don't have to. You see, even if you're done with school the Montessori model of education can still be very helpful for you. It really comes down to this: learn about different things until you find something you're passionate about and then focus your learning on that. It could be anything. But what I've found to be the most useful is not just learning facts that you can memorize (which I have done plenty of) but learning about new perspectives that really exercise your brain. The more you can challenge your mind the more you'll love learning and get something out of it too.

I believe that the best thing that you can do for your brain exercise (you're not going to like this) is to read/listen to people with different points of view. I know that sounds terrible but please hear me out. Our society, at least in America, has become much more extremist because people don't want to even imagine that there's anyone on the other side that has any good points. I personally am a moderate so I find it easier than most to listen to both sides but I admit it can be quite difficult. There are legitimately a lot of nut cases on both extremes. But there are so many people that I disagree with that sometimes do have a point.

Let me tell you a little about my experience with this. I started this process by looking up videos on Youtube by people who say happiness is overrated. As someone who's struggled for so long to achieve happiness and now has it I completely disagree but I wanted to hear the other side. And I actually have been enjoying it. A lot of what is said I find to be pretty stupid which makes me laugh. But sometimes people do bring up good points. I do agree with them that achieving happiness if you define happiness as having a lot of material things is not going to be fulfilling. I also agree that we shouldn't try to be happy 100% of the time because pushing down negative emotions rather than working through them is counterproductive.

I don't mind that there are people out there that disagree with me. We live in (what I hope is still) a free country so it's good that there are many different opinions. The problem is that we've gotten to the point where we hate each other for having different opinions. That is one of the reasons why we have gone from being classified as a full democracy to a flawed democracy. I'm fine with us not being number 1 but come on! We are supposed to be the leader of the free world! And I'm talking to both sides here: listen to different opinions. It's not going to kill you. (Thank you for listening to me rant.)

Ok now that I got that off my chest, there are other ways to stimulate your mind. There are many great speakers on Youtube that you can watch for free. There are also a lot of boring videos but eventually, you'll find your area of interest. And if you want to read a book after this one that would be good too. As I'm sure you know I'm a spiritual person so I am enjoying watching videos of people talking about God, Jesus, and the bible. I am currently into watching Rabbi Jason Sobel who is a Christian Rabbi (apparently that's a thing). But whatever you watch/listen to/read, make sure it's something that you're actually interested in and not just something people have suggested to you. Ideally, it'll make you think more deeply about things which can be a lot of fun. And that way you will earn back the love of learning that school kicked out of you!

A Human Race of Rat Racers: Let's Acknowledge This

If you've read self-help books before you likely will have heard of the term "rat racer." In case you haven't heard of this term, it means someone who is always focused on the next goal but doesn't enjoy the journey. The rat racer believes that once he, she, or they gets that promotion, gets married, has a kid, etc., they will achieve happiness. The problem is that when he, she, or they achieves a goal the happiness only lasts for a brief period of time. Not realizing the mistake in approach, the rat racer will continue to work so hard for the next goal in order to have a chance at achieving happiness. It's a vicious cycle.

But what do I mean when I say we're all rat racers (with a few exceptions). Well for the bulk of human history humans dreamed of living in a world of abundance because they were living in a world of scarcity. They wanted food to be cheap and plentiful, to not have to spend 14 hours a day working on the farm, and have material things that were just for fun. And, in the developed world, we seemed to have achieved this goal. And yet depression and anxiety rates in America are at an all-time high. But why? Well because we're still in the mindset of being rat racers. Instead of taking time to smell the roses and enjoy the accomplishments of humanity in reducing poverty, we are continuing to believe that we can't slow down and must achieve the next goal of having the biggest house, the fanciest car, or whatever material thing that we feel we need. But we also don't understand why we're like this. We hear all of the time how lucky we are to not be living in the poorest parts of the world and that makes us think "if I have so much why aren't I happy?" And this type of thinking can lead to anxiety and depression.

Why are we always thinking about the next step in life? Well, back when we were living in a world of scarcity we had to constantly be thinking about preparing for the future. If someone had a good harvest in the summer and enjoyed it rather than planning for the winter when winter came he, she, or they would starve to death. We're different from other animals in that way because they all seem to be fine once their needs are met and don't worry about the future. Now to be fair they don't talk and we can't read their thoughts so I don't know for sure that they don't think about the future but overall they do seem more chill than humans. The ability to worry about the future has led humans to advance to the top of the food chain and be rulers of this world so there are some benefits to this way of thinking. But now that we've created a world of abundance we need to focus on retraining our brains to focus more on the present.

Now retraining your brain is far from easy. And it's important to remember that getting mad at yourself just because your brain is not thinking as you would like it to is not helpful. We were born with brains that are often geared to regret the past and worry about the future. And even in modern times, there is still a need to think about these two but not nearly as much as people do. In order to quit being a rat racer it's very important to realize the importance of joy. Now joy is defined differently by different people (just like happiness) but I see joy as being in the moment and savoring the goodness of the moment. We've all had times when we were eating our favorite food but we weren't paying attention so we got very little joy out of eating. But then there are times when we focus on the food and the wonderful taste and it can bring us so much joy and happiness for the rest of the day. This applies to other things we like too.

Now I want to be very clear about the fact that just because I think people should stop being rat racers does not mean that I want to encourage people to become hedonists. In case you're not familiar with the term, a hedonist is someone who enjoys good times but never does anything they don't want to do. This may seem like a better alternative to some than being a rat racer. And in the short term, it is. It's nice to be constantly treating yourself to the yummiest food, the strongest drinks, and whatever else you may enjoy. But being a hedonist will soon enough lead to unhappiness for two reasons. The first one is obvious: if you avoid doing things you don't want to do you likely won't go to work and will end up unemployed and even broke. The second reason is less obvious. If you avoid doing anything you don't want to do you will miss out on eustress. Eustress is the good kind of stress that motivates us to be productive and enjoy the journey toward working on our goals. Hedonists do not understand this so they think that the journey toward goals has to be miserable.

It can be difficult to figure out how to be happy when you know that both being a rat racer and being a hedonist will not work for finding true happiness. At the end of the day, the solution comes down to one word: moderation. It's good to work towards goals like rat racers do but you do need to focus on enjoying the journey. It's good to enjoy good times like a hedonist but you must also still work towards goals in order to support yourself and find deeper levels of happiness. The difficult part about that is, once again, because of how our brains evolved. For thousands of years, humans have been doing things to the extreme. They had to work all day long on the farm to have any chance of feeding their families. They had to eat as much as was available to them because it was hardly ever enough. And they had to have 10 kids because they needed help on the farm and most children didn't live to turn 5. Now of course moderation would work because life has become so much more abundant. But once again, our brains are not having it. There needs to be a lot of work done by everyone to change their brains. But we must do it in moderation.

Meditation: It Works Even if You're not a Buddhist Monk

Meditation has gained a lot of popularity in the Western world over the last several years. It's actually really old though. Hindus and Buddhists have been practicing it for over 2,000 years. Buddhist monks, who meditate for hours each day, can train their bodies to do amazing things. There have even been times when monks lit themselves on fire and meditated so they didn't feel pain. Now I am not suggesting you try that but it shows that with practice meditation can enable you to do so much. And if you never get to that level, which you pretty much definitely won't, meditation can still be fun and make you feel great.

A lot of people and apps on your phone may make you feel like meditation has to be perfect. It seems like you have to be sitting cross-legged in a dark, silent room where you close your eyes and keep saying your mantra. Although this can be nice to do if you get a chance most people don't have this option. It's hard to get peace and quiet if you live with other people. Especially if those people are children. And even if you are able to meditate like this sometimes there are so many other times when you'll really need to meditate that won't allow for such a perfect setting.

I started meditating when I was 15. The first time I did it was right before bed in a dark and quiet room. It was indeed awesome. But it wasn't as great the next time I did it. And a week later I was really stressed out about something so I couldn't get my mind to focus on doing the meditation. Over the years I kept attempting to do it this way. Sometimes it would work out and I would feel amazing. But then I would start feeling stressed out again and I wouldn't be able to get my brain to focus. I couldn't figure out what I was doing wrong. Meditation is advertised as a way to decrease stress, not as something that's impossible to do when you're stressed!

It took me years to figure out how to do meditation. I kept trying to make it a habit that I did every day. Many people say that meditation each day will lower your stress levels. But for me, it'd be easy for a few days but then get harder and I would just stop. But then I found a new way to use it: to help actually deal with stress. There'd be times where I would be in public and there'd be too many people talking and that would stress me out. So I would repeat the sound "um" in my head and it would allow me to relax and zone out a bit. And no, I didn't sit down and close my eyes. I kept my eyes open and kept doing what I was doing. I didn't have to draw attention to myself. No one knew I was meditating except me.

I've continued to try out mediation for helping me in a number of ways. Earlier this year I dealt for months with being tired all of the time for no reason. I wasn't able to walk, which I love, because I was too tired. But then it finally hit me: maybe I was getting enough sleep but was not getting good quality rest. So I tried meditative walking (it's a real thing). Within a few minutes, I started feeling my energy levels rising and was able to get back to my walking routine. Meditation can really work wonders!

I believe that the reason why it took me so long to make meditation work for me is that I was going by what the experts suggested. Their recommendations may work for some but I've heard of lots of people trying meditation and quitting because it didn't work for them. It didn't work well for me at first because I was trying for perfection. I wanted to be living a life where my brain wasn't so out of control that I could just decide to stop thinking. I wanted to meditate so perfectly that I wouldn't have a single thought cross my mind the whole time. As all of my experiences with trying to be perfect have gone, that did not work in the least. The ironic thing is that meditation is not meant to be perfect or only done by perfect people. It's meant to help people with imperfect lives rest their brains so they can take a break.

You don't have to do meditation according to how Buddhist monks or I do it. Everyone's different so meditation will take trial and error to figure out. I'm sure many of you have deemed yourselves as "someone who can't do meditation." But I believe meditation can work for most people if they take the time to figure out how it can work for them. And that process will also help you find inner peace. Meditation and mindfulness are all about giving yourself a break and forgiving yourself for not being perfect. The Dalai Lama, who would be an expert at this, talks often about finding peace and loving yourself.

Once you find a way to meditate that works for you, meditation literally can change your brain. There are many different studies out there about it. Some say you have to meditate for 1 hour a day, others 20 minutes, and some even say just a few minutes a day can make a difference. Meditation has been shown to help make people more empathetic. I believe this is because it allows you to slow down your thoughts and pay more attention to people so you can understand their emotions better. It also can help shrink your amygdala. For those of you who are unaware, your amygdala is the part of the brain associated with stressful memories. It plays a large part in stress, ruminating about the past, and PTSD. I realize it's more complicated than this but basically the larger it is the more easily triggered you will become. But meditating on a regular basis has been shown to make the amygdala smaller thus reducing stress and attachment to bad memories. Not a bad deal! And even if your way of practicing meditation doesn't involve meditating every day it can still do wonders for you!

Social Media: Designed for Unhappiness

Social media has gotten a really bad rap in the regular media lately. People are upset about it selling information and in general making people feel bad. But most people may not understand the reasons why. Let's take Facebook for example. Now Facebook can be a good thing. I've actually made most of my friends through a group for adults with high-functioning autism by messaging everyone that's a part of their Facebook page. And yes I do waste time on Facebook scrolling through posts by people who mean nothing to me. But overall it has made me happier because it has allowed me to become more social. So I personally don't have any complaints but I realize that the majority, if not an overwhelming majority, of users, do.

In order to understand Facebook and other social media sites you have to understand what's the most important thing to any business: making money. As you know Facebook and other popular social media sites are free. (This may change soon with Twitter but we'll see.) Because Facebook isn't making money off of us paying monthly membership fees they acquire money through advertisers. This is done either by showing us ads or selling our information to advertisers that they can use to figure out if we're their ideal client or not. Now I don't believe showing ads in of itself is bad. A little annoying but not terrible. I, of course though am speaking as someone who hasn't bought anything I've seen in an ad in 10-15 years so clearly they're not making any money off of me. I'm not a minimalist. I just stopped seeing shopping as something fun once I was too old for toys. But that's just me. I'm not going to lecture anyone about anti-materialism.

Anyway, we now must ask ourselves what the advertisers want Facebook to do to us with their algorithms. Would the advertisers want Facebook to make us happy? Absolutely not. Why? Well, it's very simple. You're far less likely to buy a product or service that is advertised to you if you're already happy. In order to understand this we have to understand the concept behind ads. They want you to feel like a product or service will make you happy. But in order for them to convince you that you need a product or service to make you happy you need to be longing for happiness. And the further away from happiness you are the more desperate you will be to find something that will get you there.

The reason why I'm including a chapter on social media is not to say that it can't serve a purpose. There are good things about it. But because of the advertisers (who are the real customers), the algorithms do want to trigger negative emotions in you. It's important to be aware of this. It's not an accident that you're seeing so much political stuff on Facebook these days. It's one of the easiest ways to get people riled up. And getting into fights with Facebook friends you haven't seen in 20 years will not only make you be on Facebook for a longer amount of time but will also help advertisers get more information on you. There were even times, like when Cambridge Analytica collected people's data when information was used to encourage people to vote or not vote. And other social media companies have probably taken similar actions.

The reason why I'm including a chapter about how social media is purposely making most of its users unhappy is because of the huge effect it is having on our society. In the last 15 years or so social media has increasingly become a huge part of nearly everyone's life. It's used a lot more by young people though, as I'm sure you could predict. And teenage suicide rates in America have drastically gone up. This is especially true among girls. Jonathan Haidt, a social psychologist, says this is because girls are more social so they use social media sites more. It can be very difficult for people who make comparisons of themselves to others because people post about how great their lives are going even if that's inaccurate.

I also believe that social media has had a negative effect on the adults that use it. This is especially true with politics. Americans these days seem to be getting more and more extreme in their views. (I'm talking to both sides.) Social media has played a big part in this because the algorithms make it so that you only see news stories that are written from a perspective you already hold. Given, there are regular news stations that people choose to watch simply because their narrative fits the way the viewers already see the world. But the differences in what different sides get exposed to are even more extreme on social media. Not only this but social media's algorithms give more attention to long posts in the comment section which makes it so we see more users getting pissed off and getting into fights. This leads people to get more political and that leads to both sides getting more extreme.

Now, what am I proposing you do? Is there any actual point I'm trying to make? Am I telling you to quit social media altogether? I realize you're not going to quit social media just because I brought up some points that you probably have at one time or another heard before. If you're in your 20s like me it really doesn't make sense to quit social media altogether because that's how our friends communicate. It's likely even harder for teenagers in this day and age to do. But what are you supposed to do to keep these social media sites from making you unhappy? Well, you got to stop taking them so seriously. You have to realize that the influencers aren't actually happier than you, they're just pretending to be so you'll buy what they're advertising.

And also realize that people posting pictures of them having fun doesn't mean that they're happier than you, it just means that they only post the parts of their lives that are great. Now I know being aware of these facts all of the time can be difficult. It requires a lot of emotional maturity. Emotional maturity was likely stunted by social media sites. But if you can practice emotional maturity over time you'll get better at it and it will help you in many aspects of your life and not just social media. Always remember that you are the one who has the most potential to change your own brain.

Helping Others: Far From Easy But Worth It

You probably hear all the time that you should help others more. It is often implied that you are selfish if you're not using your money, power, or privilege to help the less fortunate. I used to think this way. I would get so angry about the fact that more people weren't giving to charity. I would nag family members to not only donate money to charity but to donate to charities that I gave my approval. Despite the fact that I personally didn't have much money to give I spent hours upon hours researching different charities and human welfare statistics. I was very much obsessed with it. But it took a long time for me to actually start making a difference.

There's a TED talk called "How to Be Happy Everyday" that kind of pissed me off when I saw it. Basically, the woman giving the talk said that if you do something charitable every day you'll be happy every day. I have a lot of issues with this. First of all, if you're only helping others because you expect it will make you happy you likely aren't helping anyone because you're doing it for selfish reasons. This is like when a group of young people decides to spend thousands of dollars in order to go to another country and build a school. The money they spent on travel could've paid people in these countries to build a school themselves and would've been way cheaper so they could've built multiple schools. But what these volunteers were looking for is not actually helping but having the experience that makes you feel good about yourself. If helping others guaranteed that you'd be happy every day everyone would do it. Even people who didn't give a damn about anyone else would do it because it guaranteed happiness so why not? But in reality, helping others is no easy task.

I realize I sound cynical about this subject. I want to make it clear before we go any further that I do believe (possibly even know) that it is possible to help others and when you do successfully help others it does bring happiness to you. The reason why I'm being so cynical is that I used to be so naive and I want you all to learn from your mistakes. Allow me to explain my own experiences with trying to help others. I started volunteering when I was 12. I was required to do 13 hours of community service for my Bat Mitzvah. I did my volunteer service at Jewish Family Services which is a good organization at least based on what I saw. I started out volunteering once a month by watching the kids while foster parents had a meeting in the same building. It was a lot of fun. I have always loved kids so playing with them didn't feel like work at all. I wanted to do more volunteering like this but this particular group only met once a month so I also helped stock food and asked people at the supermarket to donate food. It was a good experience.

Because I enjoyed these experiences I wanted to volunteer more. But it's very hard to find volunteer work at age 12. I assumed more opportunities would open up as I got older. When I was 16 I started volunteering for Habitat for Humanity. It's a good organization but I found it pretty boring to volunteer there. I realized that I wanted to do more volunteering that involves working with people and seeing that I helped them. Also at 16 I switched high schools and joined the charity group at my new school. The group was called One World because it raised money for international causes. I was pretty much the only one in the group who did anything so I became the president. I took pride in it and we did raise a decent amount of money but it was not without stress. It was then that I started doing lots of research into charities and poverty statistics.

I wanted to help more so I would often look up free ways to give to charity. Some things I found were legitimate because they showed ads and used the ad revenue to fund charities. But a lot of them were total gimmicks. For example, Johnson and Johnson started an app called "Donate a Photo" which would donate a dollar to the charity of your choice if you submitted a photo on the app. It took me a while to realize that this was clearly just a publicity stunt and I'm sure they donated the same amount of money either way because the photos didn't make them any money. A lot of companies and even charities do gimmicks like this too because it gives people more of the feeling that they are helping which makes the company look better. Really it's just a free way of advertising. Yay advertising!

When I went to college I was majoring in psychology because I wanted to be a therapist. I then found a site where you could volunteer as someone who listens to others' problems. It sounded perfect because it would give me experience in helping people work through their issues. It did not go so perfectly. To be fair there were some people I talked to that did feel better after talking to me and I got a lot of good reviews. But a lot of the people on the site had major anger issues and would be so mean to me. I even got sexually harassed a few times. But I wanted to help people so I kept taking breaks and then coming back to it. It was not the ideal situation.

Also while I was in college I tried to join groups that would raise money for international charities. I joined a couple but the one that stood out was the club that raised money for the charity Invisible Children. I don't know if you've heard of this one but it was a big deal in 2012 for highlighting the crimes of the Lord's Resistance Army, led by Kony, which was killing people and using child soldiers in Uganda. It sounded like a good way to help people but over time I learned more and more about the charity. Apparently, it had gotten funding from a lot of anti-gay groups in America and supported the Ugandan government even though it also used child soldiers. Also, I read the report that it was required to show the IRS and apparently less than half of the donations actually went to Uganda. It was very disheartening to see that other students were so passionate about supporting this scam. I'm certain it wasn't the only scam charity out there. I've heard of several like it.

My story of helping others does have a happy ending though. Last year I started volunteering at a hospital and did legitimately help out a few people by pushing people's wheelchairs and bringing people food. I wasn't making a huge difference but I helped a bit and enjoyed it. But then I finally found my dream opportunity. I got hired as a Recovery Support Specialist at a clinic that helped people with schizophrenia. A Recovery Support Specialist is someone who has dealt with mental illness in the past but is now in recovery and helps people who are currently dealing with mental illness. It's everything I've wanted and so much more. I love talking with people and have had so many interesting conversations even though I've only been working there for two months. So many people there have thanked me for my help. And I even get paid!

I know this chapter was pretty negative for a chapter that is about helping people. The reason why I made it this way is that I don't want to give cliched advice that doesn't actually work. Because society wants to encourage people to volunteer and donate to charity it makes it seem like all you have to do is show up or write a check and bam people will get helped. This is likely my least favorite advertising campaign for anything (and you all know how much I love advertising). In reality, helping people is hard. It's hard enough to help yourself and you have total control over yourself. So helping others that you can't control is going to be harder. But if you manage to find any way to make someone's life just a little better or easier it is worth it. I wish that I hadn't fallen for many gimmicks and forced myself to do charity work for people who were so mean to me but the job I have now is well worth all of the effort I put into searching for a way to help others. Successfully helping others is no easy task but if you manage to do it then you will indeed become much happier!

You're Allowed to be Upset: You're not going to get Kicked out of Club Happiness

You may believe that if your goal is to be happy then anytime you feel any type of negative emotion is a failure. I disagree. For example, while writing this chapter, I've been having kind of a rough day. I woke up in a bad mood for no reason so was just going to chill by scrolling through Facebook. But one thing that came up on my feed was a cat at a shelter who saw a human passing by and thought "Pick me! I'll be your best friend." But the human didn't choose this cat so the cat felt so sad. It made me think of not only animals but also humans who don't have a home and are willing to work so hard for love but still don't get it. That combined with a bad mood made me feel really down. And that's ok.

If we only ever felt happiness that would lead to a lot of messed up situations. Oh, my Mom died? Whatever. I'll just look on the bright side. Yeah, that would imply you had a really crappy relationship with your mom or are just the type of person that doesn't care about anyone. Life can be beautiful but it's also full of a lot of hardship too. For most of human history the majority of people never really even thought about being happy because life was so terrible. But in the 1700s people started thinking about it more. That's why the Declaration of Independence talks about how we have the right to the pursuit of happiness. Now I'm clearly a pro-happiness person but I recognize that it's healthy to feel negative emotions at times. Not only that but you can feel negative emotions and still be a happy person. It actually might even help with happiness because it'll make you appreciate the times you are happy more.

It's also important to remember that if someone you're talking to is going through a tough time it's really not appropriate to tell them that they should be happy. My parents have told me that back when I was really struggling they would try talking to their friends about how scared they were for me. I assume the friends they're still friends with were at least somewhat helpful but there were plenty of people that were not. People often told them that they were sure I'd get better and things would turn out alright. That was a sign to them to not bring things up with that person again. You see, not everything works out. Especially with mental health. So many people with mental health struggles never get the proper help and their stories end less than happily. This is also common for people who are physically sick. So it's really not helpful to tell someone who's suffering just to cheer up or to just not be sad. It'll make them feel that their emotions are not valid. And that's called toxic positivity.

All emotions are valid. Even when one doesn't seem like it makes sense. If you get really upset by something that you realize isn't that big of a deal it could be because it's reminding you of something that happened in the past that you still need to work on. And sometimes really bad things happen too. Yes, I do believe it is possible to eventually use the difficult times as a tool for making yourself stronger but at the moment you're not going to feel that great and that's ok. Shaming ourselves for feeling negative emotions will only, ironically, make us feel worse.

But what should you do when you feel unhappy? There's no one size fits. Sometimes talking about it with a loved one helps me. Sometimes just having a funny conversation with a stranger can work. (That's what got me out of my funk tonight). It's good to have a plan of what to do when you feel upset. I like watching my favorite movies, watching funny skits on Youtube, or trying to find a way to laugh at the situation. Laughter truly is the best medicine. But, I admit, when I'm in a bad mood I often forget about what I'm supposed to be doing. It's hard to think clearly when you're upset so try not to beat yourself up for not being able to fix the emotional problem right away.

It's important to remember that when bad things happen they will pass and get you to a point where you're feeling ok. (That is the point I am at now while writing this chapter). It's important not to let a bad time or day go to waste because it's a great learning experience. I know that may sound corny but it's true so hear me out. What I learned from today's experience is that I need to stop taking good days for granted. Most of my days are "awesome" days so when I have a "good" day I often don't enjoy it as much as I should because I've gotten so used to my days being jam-packed with good stuff. I've realized that I need to celebrate any time I have a good day by eating healthier. You see, I'm not always the healthiest eater. I eat pretty healthy at home but give into temptation a lot at the cafeteria at work. I've been struggling with this because even though I have healthy options to eat that bring me joy, they don't bring me as much joy as all the tasty food at the cafeteria does. Today I splurged a bit because I wasn't feeling good. But to be honest I often splurge on myself even when things are going well. But eating healthy can be part of the celebration of having a good day because good mental health goes well with good physical health! I don't know for sure that's going to work but I do think it shows promise. And I wouldn't have gotten to that conclusion if I hadn't had a difficult day today.

Laughter: Even Better than Medicine

Stephen Hawking once said, "life would be tragic if it weren't funny." Stephen Hawking was a famous physicist who had ALS. He spent most of his life thinking that he was going to die soon and still managed to have an amazing career and make a real contribution to the scientific world. The fact that he had such a positive outlook may shock people because of how hard his life was but to me it makes perfect sense. If you're living an easy life you don't really need a sense of humor. Yes, you may enjoy sitcoms or funny movies but real comedy is tragedy plus timing. Laughter allows us to take the stress in life and not only stop it from physically hurting us but to turn it into something that makes us feel so good.

When people suggest that you should laugh more they often say you should find something funny to watch. The problem with that is that it can be very hard as an adult to find a show that's genuinely funny. Once when I went to a conference about happiness and the brain with my dad the instructor explained to us that in order to create a joke you need a punchline that is both unexpected and makes sense. The example he used was "what do engineers use for birth control? Their personalities." That made me laugh. But oftentimes sitcoms do the same kind of joke that's been done to death on other shows so it's not unexpected. Or oftentimes the punchline on these shows doesn't make any sense.

A good sitcom is not easy to find but I don't believe it's what's meant to be our best option for a laugh. I believe the 2 best times to laugh are when things go wrong and when you notice one of your flaws. Now you may be thinking "why would I laugh at bad situations and my own flaws? Aren't those bad things?" Well, you've answered your own question. The real purpose of laughter (not the only purpose but the most important one) is to make the difficult parts of life not only bearable but actually enjoyable. It's one of the most powerful things we can do because if we can make the difficult times bring us joy then what can't bring us joy?

Now it's very important that when you do laugh you're not laughing at someone's expense. If someone tells you that they're really struggling it's not appropriate to just tell them to laugh at it. They have to decide on their own. But if it's your situation, laughter can do wonders. It not only relieves short term stress but will make you much less afraid of the bad thing happening again because you know that you can get something good out of it. This will enable you to take more risks at different things you may not be good at right away because things not working out will not scare you so much. It takes practice, I know it does. But eventually it'll start happening on its own. No longer will you have to tell yourself to try to find the funny part of the situation because your body will learn to start laughing as soon as your mood drops.

Laughter is also fantastic at helping you accept yourself for not being perfect. We all have flaws even if some people refuse to admit theirs. (And these types of people pretend they're perfect because they can't accept their real selves.) And that's ok. Flaws make us human. But it can be so hard if you insist on beating yourself up just because you are flawed in many ways. But if you can laugh at your flaws it will relieve so much self-hatred. You are the star of your own sitcom. You mess up and say the wrong things but that's what makes the show interesting. And you have a front-row seat to get to know everything about the show and get to laugh all you want. Seeing it this way will help you not take life, and yourself, so seriously.

Now you may think that if you laugh at your flaws you'll be less likely to improve upon them. But, at least in my experience, laughter can help with that. For example, I can be really lazy and take forever to take out the trash. But when I joked about how I'm failing at adulting it relieved the stress I had around taking out the trash and so I was able to do it. Yes, it is a little sad I had to figure out a way to get myself to simply take out the trash. And I laugh about that too!

Our society (at least in America) has been teaching people to take things so seriously. The self-esteem movement has taught kids that they're perfect and anyone who says anything otherwise is a terrible person. The art of laughing at yourself seems to be becoming more and more of a lost art. Self-esteem is good but in order for you to really have high self-esteem you have to have high self-compassion. Self-compassion means that you forgive yourself for not being perfect. Laughing at yourself can be very helpful with this because it shows you that it's not so bad to be imperfect. It can even be fun. And there's nothing wrong with being imperfect. Any human who claims to be perfect either is lying about being perfect or lying about being human. See! This is a perfect example of a joke that cracks me up whether or not anyone reading this actually understood it!

Another way to use humor to numb the pain of life is to laugh at politicians. Yes, politics can be stressful to talk about because everyone has become so polarized. But comedy can bring people of all worldviews together. Some people believe that the main point of laughter is to unite us. I believe there are other important purposes too but uniting people together is a great thing. When I was 14 and had just started therapy I soon learned that my therapist had the opposite political views of mine. But that wasn't an issue because we had fun with it. We would make fun of each other which actually brought us closer together. And I enjoyed being a little obnoxious (when discussing politics it's hard not to be). But it was all in good fun. If people on both sides of the political spectrum can laugh together people will learn to stop hating the other side. And they'll have a great time doing it!

Don't Look for Shortcuts: This Book Isn't Going to Fix your Life on its Own

Ok, so I have to address this. If you're still reading this book at this point, congrats you're more than halfway through. I assume if you're still reading this book you think it has some real insights that can help improve your life. If so, I am very glad that you've learned some new material. But please, for all that is good in the world, don't get excited. This book WILL NOT be a shortcut to happiness. Doing even just one of the things I've suggested is going to take A LOT of work.

Let's look at my first tip: gratitude. Unless you've never read a self-help book before, and even if you didn't, I'm sure you've heard about the power of gratitude. But then why haven't you achieved it? Because it's freaking hard. Our brains didn't evolve to be grateful. You have to literally retrain your brain to be grateful when it's made for greed. It is doable but it's by no means an easy task. I don't want you to fall into the trap that most people who read self-help books or listen to motivational speakers fall into. The trap I am referring to is the trap of excitement. You may think to yourself "wow now I know the secret to happiness" and be so excited that every day of your life is going to be awesome from now on. You'll go to sleep so excited to start the first day of the rest of your life. And then you actually try being grateful, or any of the tips I suggested, and it doesn't work out perfectly on your first try so you lose all hope, curse me for making you feel false excitement, and feel less happy than you did before reading the book.

It's possible my book may have caused you to fall into this excitement trap and for that, I apologize. I hope you believe me when I say that getting you to fall into this trap was my intention with this book. But a lot of people who preach "how to be happy" kind of do. Motivational speakers will say nice sounding stuff like "you can achieve anything" and "follow these steps and you'll achieve the perfect you!" Now that stuff is nice to hear and if you went to the event in person you probably enjoyed the event very much because of the high level of energy in the room. But is it actually going to change your life? Probably not. Why? Because finding the answer to happiness involves more than just nice-sounding motivational sentences. But because they make people feel good, people will keep going back to these events (and spend quite a bit for them).

Once again I ruined something fun for you with my cynicism. Yeah I'm doing that on purpose. I want you to have a realistic view of the world. I think I do. I am an extremely happy person but I'm also cynical. I don't see why those two can't go together. That's why this book has a hell of a lot more cynicism than most self-help books (not all but most). I want you to realize that this book is not meant to be a quick fix. Or something that tells you the world is perfect and amazing all of the time if you just have the right attitude. It's a book that I hope will point you in the right direction towards achieving happiness. Not something that will achieve happiness for you. Happiness takes a lot of work. Not only achieving it but also maintaining it. But so many people love the self-help industry because they're looking for a shortcut to happiness.

Am I saying there is no shortcut to happiness? No, because I don't know everything about it and there may be some people out there who have found it. But those people are hard to find because there's thousands if not millions of people that claim to have found it. It's tempting to want a shortcut. If you have a bacterial infection and go to a doctor most of the time they'll give you antibiotics and boom after 2 weeks you're cured. So why can't happiness be like that? Well because very few things in life are. Even with the antibiotics example it's more complex than that because some doctors prescribe antibiotics for viral infections which can cause antibiotic resistance. I'm not saying that it's fair that life is far more complicated than just taking a pill or getting an easy answer but it is. But it's human nature to want it to be. And I don't blame anyone for that. Back when I was depressed I would spend a lot of time looking up "cures for depression/anxiety." I didn't want to suffer anymore so I thought I needed to find something to save me.

Now, it is true that I did receive help with my depression and mania with medication but it was not a quick fix. I had to spend 9 years trying out so many different drugs, many that came with side effects, before I found the right ones for me. And even then the pills helped heal my brain a bit but I still wasn't happy. But I had gratitude because I was grateful to not be depressed any longer. And over time I worked hard to add other good things to my life such as friends and family. I am very blessed but it did take a lot of work. And that's ok.

It's exhausting to try so many things and have them not work out. Especially when the goal is to be happy. Life is very hard to deal with without happiness. I'm not promising you that if you roll up your sleeves and work hard to implement the tips I've included in this book then things will definitely work out. Happiness is something that requires a lot of trial and error. And some people can achieve it easily while many cannot. For some it may be so close to impossible. I do believe that with the right tips and amount of hard work anyone can achieve at least some happiness. But I could easily be wrong. It's not like I can test that out on 8 billion people. I'm not here to give you false hope. I do hope that my story and these tips will help you but I can't guarantee they will. No one can honestly promise you that either and I believe honesty, even when it's shitty, is the best approach for me to take in this book. But what I can promise you is that if you do achieve becoming a happy person it will be so much better than you ever imagined. That's the one promise to you I'll make.

The Prosperity Gospel: Not my Kind of God

So first of all I'd like to provide a little background on my religiosity because I feel that will help me explain things better in this chapter. I am a Jewish Christian. But I'm not half and half I'm 100 100. I was born Jewish to a completely Jewish family. I went to Hebrew school and had a Bat Mitzvah. I take a lot of pride in the accomplishments and endurance of Jews throughout history and very much identify as a Jew. I never thought that I was going to become a Christian too. It happened kind of unexpectedly. In college I joined a friend to go to a Christian dinner because it was free so why not? That's the Jew in me. (I'm allowed to say it). I ended up really liking the discussion they had about God's love that is shown throughout the bible so I decided to go again the next week. I ended up going every week for the rest of my Junior year and most of my Senior year. I really enjoyed the discussions.

After college, I struggled with finding the right church to go to. So many of them had such boring services and the people seemed judgmental. Eventually, shortly after I started my process of recovery from mental illness, I found a great church that was just a 3 minute walk away from my apartment. They are so wonderful and loving and the services have a lot of singing during them. But I still struggled with my relationship with God and Jesus. I wanted a closer relationship but I was still afraid that they hated me because of me having to deal with mental illness for so long. But eventually I started to see that God did love me and Jesus didn't regret his sacrifice for me because my suffering eventually led to many good things happening in my life.

Ok now that I explained my religious background let me explain why I am very critical of the prosperity gospel. In case you don't know, the prosperity gospel is an interpretation of the bible that some preachers preach that states that all you have to do is believe in God (and maybe do some good work) and your life will be filled with blessings. Sounds nice, doesn't it? But that's just it; it sounds nice but doesn't hold any weight. If all you had to do was praise God and boom your life would be perfect then why would anyone have any doubt in God's existence? No one would be able to deny the existence of God if it was that simple to get God to give you what you want. And why would there still be suffering among very religious people? So many people nowadays stop believing in God when something bad happens to them or a loved one of theirs because if they praised God why would this have happened to them?

If God only brought good things to you as long as you praised him and his son then having a good relationship with God would be easy. He'd be like your servant or errand boy who was always on top of getting you whatever you wanted because you are just so special. Now if you don't believe in God (which is fine) you may not have realized this but having a good relationship with God is far from easy. Believing in and praising God by no means guarantees your life is going to be easy. I tried forming a closer relationship with God back when I was depressed because I thought it would help the depression. I stayed depressed for a long time so I felt that God really hated me. At the time I did listen to some religious leaders on Youtube who talked about the prosperity gospel. I would watch the video and it would make me feel good for a bit but this always generous God who would make everything perfect never did appear to me. I kept trying to figure out what horrible sin I had committed that caused God to hate me because I thought that if I was a good person God would have relieved me of depression.

Now I'm not an expert on God and I'm not claiming to be. Honestly I don't think there really is such a thing as being an expert on God. But that's a theory for another day. But what I've found through my experience with connecting to God is that I can't just order him around. Just because I go to church, praise God, and do my best to help his children by no means I can just tell him what I want and he'll always bring it to me. That's not God. That's Santa Claus. And Santa is only meant for children for a reason. We all have plans for how we want our lives to go but really it's God who decides the plan and we must do our best to make the most of what life God has given us whether we like God's choice or not. It's not up to us. But as I've learned to trust more in God and make the best of the difficulties he sends my way rather than trying to fight his plan, my life has improved tremendously. Yes, I do have a lot of good things in my life now but there's still difficult days. I'm actually having one right now. But I'm doing my best to make the best of it rather than fighting it. And it's actually turning out ok.

Why do preachers preach the prosperity gospel? A lot of them may do it in order to make you want to buy their books or donate to their salary. But some may not be trying to get anything out of it. They may just honestly believe that praising God will always improve your life because that may have been their experience. There's a saying that holds true: never trust a leader who walks without a limp. If your pastor/priest/rabbi has never struggled in life and especially in their relationship with God I highly recommend that you find someone new to listen to. Life is hard for almost everyone and some people have been from hell and back. But those who've been through horrible times and still praise God know that praising God is not easy but still worthwhile. They will know that God doesn't magically solve all of your problems the second you ask him to but he will always be on your side while you get through these difficult times offering his love and support. God's love, even if it doesn't come with blessings, is the real goal you should be trying to achieve and hopefully you have a religious leader that preaches that type of gospel.

Happiness Capitalism: A Term Either I or Someone Smarter Made Up

So before I begin this chapter I would like to acknowledge that just the word "capitalism" brings up a lot of feelings for many people. I'm sure you'd like to know whether I'm pro or anti-capitalist. The thing is I'm going to piss off people on both sides because I do believe capitalism has both good and bad parts to it. I very much like that capitalism has brought nearly the entire world out of poverty. You see back in the year 1800 (shortly after Adam Smith wrote about capitalism) 85-94% of the world was living in what we would now consider extreme poverty. Now that number's down to 10% so clearly, capitalism has made a big dent. But there are also things about capitalism I'm not the biggest fan of. It encourages consumerism which I have some issues with (see my many references to my opinions on advertising). But whether you like capitalism or not I do believe it is the system we have with happiness so hopefully, you will continue reading this chapter.

So you've probably heard the term often applied to capitalism: "the rich get richer and the poor get poorer." This is partially true for happiness capitalism as well. The way happiness capitalism works is that you can take your happiness and invest it in getting things and experiences that will make you happier. Back when I finally got on the right medication I was still very unhappy but I now had a tiny bit of happiness because I was grateful to have a chance at feeling joy again. I invested that in different things that made me happier and thus gave me more happiness to invest. I joined a church, I repaired my relationship with family members, and I joined a group for adults with high-functioning autism where I made so many great friends just to name a few.

Allow me to better explain the concept of happiness capitalism through two stories. First we'll start with a story that explains how happiness capitalism is a great thing and then I'll do a story about its limitations. I know everyone has their own views on financial capitalism but please read each story with an open mind.

Callie is not a very happy person. She doesn't get joy from many things. The only part of her day that she does enjoy is when she watches her favorite comedy movies at night because they make her laugh. But one day Callie reads this book or something more meaningful and decides to start investing her happiness. After she finishes watching a funny movie that night she decides to not spend the rest of the night going on social media and ruining her good mood by getting pissed off by things others have posted. Instead, she uses the happy energy she has gotten from the funny movie to find a funny article online. It takes a while to find a good one so it's very helpful to her that she's in a good mood from the movie. But eventually, she finds a few sites with really funny articles. She spends the whole night laughing and gets much more high quality sleep because she goes to bed feeling so good.

The next day Callie wakes up feeling pretty good but then remembers that it's a Monday so she has to go to her job that she really dislikes. She's a little upset at first but then realizes that she does want to do more to invest her happiness. So she decides to try to appreciate her job. She realizes that she wouldn't be able to afford her apartment without her job. And yes her apartment isn't the nicest but it is very quiet and allows her to relax and have a good laugh. This wouldn't be possible without the paycheck she gets from her job. She leaves for work in a slightly better mood about it. Because she's feeling a little better at work she decides to put that energy towards coming up with compliments for her coworkers. She tells one of her coworkers, Amy, that she always admires how Amy comes into work dressed so nicely. Amy, who had never been a friend to Callie before, thanks Callie and during lunch break offers Callie a homemade chocolate chip cookie from the ones she had brought into work for herself. The cookie is delicious which makes Callie even happier. And she especially appreciates that Amy returned the favor of being nice.

Over the next several months Callie keeps investing in her happiness. Now to be fair, not all of her investments pay off. A few of the coworkers she compliments continue to be rude to her. But overall her happiness investments pay off nicely. She befriends several of her coworkers because she puts in the effort of being nice like she was to Amy. She starts getting along with her family much better because she calls her parents once a week and tells them that she loves them instead of going on and on about how they screwed her childhood up. And she gets promoted because she puts more effort into doing her work assignments. Callie has truly become a very successful happiness capitalist.

I hope you found the last story uplifting but unfortunately happiness capitalism does have its downsides. Let's look at the story of Maddie. Maddie was decently happy for the first 19 years of her life but then she developed a mental illness and became extremely depressed. Despite the fact that many people view those suffering from mental illness as lazy, Maddie tries so hard to become at least a little bit happy. She tries doing the things she usually enjoys but they're just too painful. You see, when someone has clinical depression (and I don't mean had a bad day I mean actual clinical depression) usually can't get joy out of anything. And not only does Maddie not feel joy while doing these activities but she starts to feel even worse because she's so upset that nothing she once found fun she enjoys anymore. Maddie also tries going through the motions by continuing to go to her college classes and part time job. But the racing thoughts in her head made it impossible for her to concentrate. She ends up failing out of school and getting fired from her job for crying in front of others. Because of this she has to move home. Her parents, who are usually supportive, don't understand what's going on with her mental illness and don't know what to do. They sign her up for therapy but it doesn't seem to be working. Eventually Maddie can't handle all of the fighting going on between her and her family so she leaves home and now lives in a tent in the park. A very sad story.

I know that was depressing so I'll add a happy ending. Maddie eventually finds a homeless shelter that specializes in helping young people with mental illness. They provide her with a place to sleep, therapy, and psychiatric appointments. It takes a long time but eventually Maddie is able to overcome her depression and start working on becoming happy again. There are many people with mental illness that will not receive this help but hopefully over time more people will.

Now you're probably wondering what my overall view on happiness capitalism is when I just shared how it can be wonderful or horrific. Well I think it's a complex thing. It's hard to know by just meeting someone who is unhappy if they are dealing with something clinical or are just a lazy happiness capitalist. My advice would be not to judge people so quickly. Just like, although I believe financial capitalism can be an amazing thing, it's not fair to just assume beggars are lazy. It's not a perfect system. But if you are blessed to be a successful happiness capitalist (and yes it's a blessing because it does involve luck) I believe that you should try to find a way to help others who haven't been able to achieve what you've achieved. I'm not trying to guilt you into doing anything, I just want you to be a little more understanding. Whatever your situation is, assuming your brain's working properly, there is always a possibility you could become a successful happiness capitalist but please don't judge others for not achieving the happiness dream.

The One Right Path Doesn't Exist: You Have to be Open Minded About the Future

They say you have to "live in the moment" and most of the time that's true. But there are times when we do need to think about the future. The problem is so many of us spend too much time not only thinking about the future but planning out every little detail. I'm not getting down on anyone because I've been a prime example of this. When I was a kid I was constantly thinking about the future because my life was pretty boring. I imagined getting married, having a whole lot of kids, and being a stay-at-home mom. I spent so much time planning what I was going to name my kids and how I would raise them. I pictured this as a life that would make me very happy.

As I got older I started to imagine myself having a career. When I was 16, after being in therapy for 2 years, I decided I wanted to be a therapist so I could help people with depression. It seemed like a good path for me and for years I seemed to be moving closer to my goal. I went to a college known for psychology (Clark University) where I majored in psychology. I was accepted into a few different high ranked schools to get a masters in social work at. I was planning on attending Fordham University. But God had other plans for me.

You see, during my junior year of college, I thought that things were going very well. I seemed so happy and everyone thought that I was. But in reality, I was experiencing the manic part of bipolar and, as what always happens, I crashed. It was a horrible summer but luckily I was able to go back and complete my degree. But my parents realized that I was in no shape to be attending graduate school. And I was PISSED. I couldn't believe that they were taking away my dream. I just couldn't see any way I could possibly be happy unless I achieved my dream of going to graduate school. This went on for 5 years. I actually changed my mind about what type of graduate school I wanted to go to but I was absolutely certain that getting a master's would be my only chance at getting a job where I could become self-sufficient. I just couldn't get myself to see any other way.

At the time me writing this book, I still have not attended graduate school. And I am perfectly happy about that. I now have a job as a Recovery Support Specialist that has truly become my dream job. I get to help people every day and I have so much fun with it. And it pays decently. The job doesn't even require a college degree though. Which is fine. I've realized that only God knew what the right path for me was and I am so glad about how it all worked out. It's impossible to know exactly what path you should take so you just have to capitalize on the opportunities you end up getting.

So many kids today are led to believe there is only one acceptable path to career success: going to college. Most of the material taught in k-12 education in public schools are meant for the sole purpose of comparing kids for college. Fewer and fewer high schools still teach trades to kids because it may lower their math and reading skills that they'll need if they go to college. Now to be clear, I'm not saying college is useless. I went to college and I'm now working in the field that I majored in. And of course we need college in order to have doctors, lawyers, engineers, and many other necessary professions. But college isn't meant for everyone. 43% of college students end up dropping out for a variety of reasons which means that they incur debt without even getting a degree out of it. And even if people graduate from college it's not always helpful in finding a job. So many college students end up underemployed because the rate of young people graduating from college is going up at least twice as fast as the rate of jobs that require a college degree are being created. Economies take time to change and we need more than just doctors, lawyers, and engineers. We need plumbers, electricians, and welders too. Trade school should be seen as a great option for high school graduates who don't want to spend 4 years incurring massive amounts of debt. But we shame those in these fields. We act like the only reason to go into the trades is because you're too dumb for college. And yes, those who go to college tend to have better math and reading skills than those who go into the trades but that's not the most important thing. What is important is being able to land a good job that both pays enough to live on and is enjoyable without having to pay an arm and a leg first.

So many people get obsessed with planning every last detail about their futures that they sacrifice happiness in the present with no actual benefit for the future. You may have imagined becoming a doctor and making tons of money when you were growing up. But then you find out that the pre med courses are ridiculously hard and getting through medical school is even harder so your dream doesn't work out. Or maybe you do manage to become a doctor but you absolutely hate it. It can be very difficult to let go of the plans you had for the future. You may feel like you're a failure and you're doomed to a life of unhappiness. But happiness isn't about getting everything you want for your future. It's about enjoying the future you do achieve. Maybe the doctor thing doesn't work out but you find another profession that you most like and make a decent living at. That may just be what God (or the universe) intended for you. And enjoying it doesn't make you a failure in the slightest. It makes you a successful happiness capitalist.

You've probably heard the saying "want to make God laugh? Tell him your plans." This really is true. None of us know what's going to happen in the future. At the time of me writing this it's still been less than 3 years since I've been feeling good. 3 years ago I was so depressed that I couldn't get joy out of anything. I just wanted to get through each day and I barely was able to. I could've never dreamed of being an extremely happy person with a great job. And yet, 3 years later, I am. If I was the planner of my life it wouldn't be anywhere near as awesome as God has made it. So I'm ok with not being completely in charge. God wants amazing things for all of us. And it's ok if that doesn't line up with your plans.

Child of God not Expert on God

As you have picked up on by now, I am a very spiritual person. My relationship with God is very important to me and connecting with God more has very much improved my life. But I am not an expert on God's plan for humanity and honestly I don't think anybody is. Now when it comes to people struggling with God I don't think it's so much about whether or not someone believes in God. Those who do believe in God tend to be confident in their belief. And the same goes for those who do not believe in God. But the big question that makes those who believe in God struggle and those who don't believe in God stay away from even the thought of him is, you guessed it, "why does God allow bad things to happen to good people?" It may be the earliest question people have had about him. And I am no expert on that.

The reason why I'm discussing this in this book is because I want you to know that believing in God isn't an easy path or something that will automatically make you feel better. As one of my college friends used to say about relationships with God, "if it's easy you're not doing it right." Just like pretty much everyone I have struggled with this particular question. At first the question was "why did God make so many bad things happen to me when I hadn't done anything wrong?" Over time I've been able to find a lot of meaning in my suffering and am very blessed to have been able to. But I can't speak for other people. I'm not going to say that "life is what you make of it" applies to everyone. I do believe it applies to me but I know that there are so many hard working people out there that just never catch a break. Not to mention the fact that 5 million children in the world die every year before their 5th birthday. It's definitely too complicated to figure out.

Now you've probably heard religious people say "bad things happen because God gave humans free will." But that only accounts for the bad things that are caused by humans. Not to mention the fact that it brings up the question of why so many bad people get put into positions of power in the first place. Yes in a democracy they're voted in but for most of human history there were no democracies and the emperors and monarchs got to rule the whole country simply because they were born into the position of power. And even if the free will argument may explain why humans do bad things to other humans it doesn't explain why there's so many diseases in the world or why there's starvation. For most of human history the life expectancy was 30 at best because of disease and starvation. We have made a lot of progress in that regard but there's still millions of children who die because of those.

While writing this chapter I looked up the question "why do bad things happen to good people" in order to see what I could find from a Christian perspective. I found an interesting perspective by C.S. Lewis who was a famous Christian and the author of "The Lion, the Witch, and the Wardrobe." He talks about how goodness of God is more than just about God giving us what we want and what will make us happy. Sometimes God causes us pain because "pain is a sharp, clear tool to achieve purpose." I have mixed feelings about this. I do believe that the pain I suffered from did point me in the right direction. It took years and I had no idea when I was feeling the pain that it may actually have purpose at the time. But 3 years later I have learned so much and have gained more happiness than I ever thought possible. But I don't want to be one of those people that assume that because everything worked out for me with hard work that anyone who isn't living the life is in that position because they're stupid or lazy.

There is something to be said for hard times making you stronger. I personally don't believe the hard times themselves make you stronger but how you take advantage of them once they're over. Now I know I talk a lot about how the tough times made me stronger but I realize that while they were going on they made me weaker. It wasn't until at least a year after my life became good that I saw that maybe they had a purpose. I really did believe for a long time that God hated me. When you're suffering your brain often doesn't work so well. You're so overwhelmed with just getting through the day that you can't focus enough on figuring out the lessons of this tough time. And when I say a rough time I don't mean having one bad day. I mean really truly suffering.

I also realize that so many people never get the chance to learn from their suffering. For a lot of people, health is something they have but don't appreciate until they get old and lose their health. And by then it's too late to appreciate the health they once had because usually the health problems just keep getting worse until death comes. And then there are also so many kids who die young. How are they supposed to figure out the meaning of their suffering during such short lives? And there's also plenty of people who live a long life but have terrible things going on nonstop so they never get the chance to relax and really think about the meaning of their own suffering. "What doesn't kill you makes you stronger" doesn't apply to everyone by any means whatsoever.

I guess what this chapter is really about is that humans are never going to fully understand God and we shouldn't try to push our interpretations of God on others. Certain questions don't have exact answers that we're meant to know. Maybe all of everyone's suffering is for the best. Maybe children die because they were chosen to go to Heaven faster. I don't know. And that's ok. It's alright to admit that you don't have all of the answers. It's ok to really struggle with figuring out how an almighty and all-loving God could allow certain bad things to happen to good people. It's an uncomfortable feeling to believe that but life can be uncomfortable and scary at times. And believing in God may be too much for you if something really horrible has happened to you or a loved one. I'm not even saying that having a relationship with God is the universal best choice. But if you do attempt to have a relationship with God please remember that it in no way guarantees that you'll have all of the answers to life's hardest questions.

Everyone (and I do mean everyone) Needs to Calm the Hell Down

Both sides of the political aisle are more and more treating the other side like they are evil. If you're stupid enough like me to still be watching the news you probably see this happening over and over again. Each side paints the other side as villains with no redeeming qualities whatsoever. This, of course, makes people on both sides so angry. How could you not be angry when evil is lurking? But since both sides think the other side is evil there's not much room for compromise. And it's causing most of the country to be scared of anyone with different political beliefs. That makes us more polarized so much so that many people are talking about how America may have a second civil war.

How do we stop our country (assuming you're an American) from crumbling apart? Well, in order to understand that we must understand the different aspects of human nature. So there are the most basic brain functions such as anger and fear. Anger and fear are both playing a big part in everyone's lives these days. You see, back when we were cave people our brains were not nearly as advanced. We could only handle basic emotions. So if we saw a lion headed toward us we would automatically feel fear and that feeling would get us to run away for our lives. It made sense back when the world was full of things that were constantly trying to kill us. But over time our brains have evolved so we are capable of having more complex emotions. But still, so many people fall prey to these basic emotions because the more complex ones take work to develop.

Allow me to explain with a short story. This story is about twins Devin and Hayden. Devin doesn't like to put much effort into developing complex emotions. So when she overhears her coworkers talking badly about her she gets so angry that she goes right up to them and calls them all bitches and whores. As you can predict this doesn't end particularly well. After getting a warning from her boss about her behavior she knows that she shouldn't act this way at work but the next time it happens she goes with her anger again and ends up getting fired. Hayden takes a different approach. When she hears her coworkers talking badly about her she feels angry just like Devin did. But instead of letting the anger take over her brain, she decides to spend the next few minutes taking deep breaths. This calms down her body's anger response. It allows her to calmly tell the other coworkers that she can overhear them talking and doesn't appreciate what they are seeing and will report it to HR if it continues. It does continue so she reports it to HR and the coworkers end up getting punished instead of her. And even if they didn't she at least still has her job.

Now let's put Devin and Hayden in a different situation. They both have the same political beliefs. One day they are at a party and someone there who has the opposite political beliefs as them starts talking about politics. Devin gets angry and tells this person to shut the hell up and that she's a horrible person for thinking that way. Devin ends up having to leave the party. That night she takes out her anger by sending mean messages to people who disagree with her on social media. Hayden takes a different approach. She calmly explains to this woman who disagrees with her why she disagrees. At first, the woman gets defensive but Hayden assures this person that she's not trying to belittle her but is actually interested in having a political discussion and learning about where this woman is coming from with her beliefs. They end up having an hour-long discussion and both leave feeling like they still have the same beliefs but understand the other side just a little bit better.

Now of course it is not always that easy. But the point I'm trying to make is that if we allow anger and fear to control us then we're never going to make anything political any better. I'm a moderate but I do have political preferences. I'm not going to go into which ones but I will tell you that I do try to watch videos on Youtube that present opinions on both sides of the aisle. It can be difficult to do at times especially because both sides are so angry and angry people make me angry. But sometimes hearing a different perspective does get me to see things a little differently. Or at least shows me that the other side may be coming from at least a decent place.

You see the more hatred we have for one side the more hatred they're going to have for us. Yelling at people is not going to change anyone's beliefs. It likely will just make them hate your side more. But if we can try to actually listen it could bring us closer together even if we do still disagree. You see, if we're ever going to improve the government at all we need to start with the individual. If individuals can't be willing to listen to one another, how can we possibly expect politicians (who are always going to be worse than the average person) to? Now yes, I do believe there are people out there that legitimately want evil things. But it's NOT half the country. But anger blinds us so that's how so many of us see things nowadays. So take a deep breath and maybe we all might just survive. Maybe.

Seeing the Best in Kids

People are constantly talking about how the younger generation is so terrible. For a while, they were talking about Millenials (my generation) but now they've moved on to getting so upset with Gen Z. Older adults feel like children are so spoiled and won't work hard enough like older generations did as young adults. But what if we looked at children in a way that assumed the best? A way where rather than blaming them for their shortcomings we try to help them overcome those shortcomings. I believe that this must start before children grow up and go off to college because then it won't have much of an effect. We have to look at the childhood kids these days are having and try to see what we can do to allow it to turn them into happy, responsible adults.

Let's look at what is a huge factor in a young child's life: school. Most kids these days start preschool when they are 2 or 3 and nearly all will stay in school until they are high school graduates. After that many will continue school in order to get a Bachelor's. And master's and Ph.D. programs are becoming more popular as well. But I will just be focusing on talking about K-12 education for now. Now it is very well known that something is wrong with the K-12 education system. Some say we need school choice. Some say we need better teachers. But, at least how it seems to me, the most obvious question we should be asking about K-12 education is: are kids actually learning anything?

If you have kids or just remember being a kid you probably realize that school is not doing a good job at all at teaching kids anything useful about the world. If you ask adults if they learned anything in high school that actually has helped them with their job so few of them will say no. Now some people say that school may not teach you much useful information but it teaches you how to think. But does it? I don't believe that memorizing useless information in order to pass a test and then forgetting all of it right after the test is a good way to teach kids how to think.

Now I do believe even wealthy kids are disadvantaged by the system but it is true that lower-income kids have it worse. In a study done a few years ago, researchers rated which factors had the biggest impact on how children did in school. The biggest was parental involvement. The next two were socioeconomic status and maternal education. So…nothing to do with the school itself. This is because students are not being taught to love learning and enjoy the benefits that come from learning itself. Instead, we tell them that learning useless information is important because it will allow them to get an A+ on the test. But a grade isn't going to naturally mean anything to a 5-year-old because they can't look ahead to getting into college if it's at least 13 years away. Instead what matters to a child is if their parents are angry or proud of them. If a parent tells a child that they will get ice cream if they get an A and will be grounded if they get an F then children will likely work hard to get an A. But if the parent is too busy trying to make ends meet and isn't very involved in their children's education then the child will think that grades are just meaningless letters on a piece of paper. And can you really blame them?

But the education system does work for wealthy kids with involved parents, right? I do not believe so. I grew up in an upper-middle-class neighborhood that had a top-rated public school system. I did well in school academically because I was very good at sitting still, being quiet, and memorizing useless information. I valued grades a lot because I had low self-esteem and getting straight A's gave me a self-esteem boost. But I would get so stressed out about grades. I felt that if I wasn't getting all A's I was failing at life. So many kids feel very stressed out about school. But if I was taking a class that I enjoyed I would be perfectly fine with working harder and it wouldn't feel like hard work. Most students feel the same way. And yet we just assume that they're lazy if they're not studying their hardest at classes they hate.

Now I know when people complain about our education system they usually don't have a solution in mind. I mean, they may suggest putting more money into education but that hasn't really made a difference. America spends more per student than any other country in the world and yet in world rankings our students score just average in reading and science and below average in math. It's possible more money could help but clearly just throwing money at the problem is not getting us anywhere. But what would it be like for a child to go to a school where they're not only actually learning something but are able to focus on learning goals in areas that actually interest them? Well, there is a solution that's been around for decades: Montessori schools.

The basic idea behind Montessori schools is that children learn best when they can develop skills in areas that interest them and do so through play. If children can learn through play they won't find it boring and will really enjoy the process. Because let's be real: children love learning. From the day they are born, they are constantly learning new things about the world. That's why babies sleep so much. They're learning so much that they need to give their brains a rest. And 90% of brain development happens in the first 5 years of life so it's a great time to learn all that you can. And yet we assume kids don't like learning because they don't like school. But if the school offered a fun way of learning, as it should, kids would be unstoppable in learning so much more than we ever did in school.

Now you probably have a few questions about this if you're a parent, as you should. If you've heard of Montessori education you may have heard that most Montessori schools are just for preschool and kindergarten. You may not think older kids can learn through the Montessori system. It is true that the inventor of Montessori schools, Dr. Maria Montessori, only figured out how it would work up through grade 6. But there are a few Montessori high schools that allow kids to learn through apprenticeships and may even give them funding for starting their own businesses. Even if these opportunities don't lead to a career for the teenagers, which they might, they still are a lot more interesting than regular high school and will teach teenagers the value of hard work and creativity.

Now you may also be asking yourself how this will prepare students for college. The way most schools work is to be as much like college as they can. They require students to take lots of tests and write lots of papers because that's what the students will have to do in college. What if Montessori schools don't prepare schools for this? First of all, we as a society really need to realize that college isn't for everyone. 43% of college students drop out which means they get into massive amounts of debt without even getting a diploma. And things for recent college graduates aren't much better. 41% of students who graduated from college within the last two years are working at a job that doesn't require a college degree. Not going to college would've allowed them an extra 4 years of full-time work experience which would likely have helped them much more in the job market and without having to go into debt. But even if a child does want to pursue a job in a field that requires a college degree they shouldn't have to choose between going to college and actually learning something. A Montessori education would allow them to learn both what they enjoy doing and what they are good at which will be a huge help in getting them to decide on a major and a career path. And it may also allow them to get a good job without going to college because college itself should not be the goal. Getting a job they love should be.

But what if Montessori school doesn't prepare students for the real world? The fact is that many jobs have the same problems as traditional education systems: they're unfulfilling. So many people have jobs that they can't stand and continue to work there only because they need the money. Where would they have learned that life has to be this way? Traditional education schools. If we teach kids that life is full of just having to do useless tasks for extrinsic goals then they'll assume that having a job is not about enjoying it or achieving something good for society but just going through the motions in order to get a paycheck just like students are taught to just suck it up in order to get a good grade. But what if it didn't have to be this way? What if students were excited to get up on the first day of school rather than the last? What if students loved learning so much that they were sad when it came time for summer vacation? What if they were willing to work their butt off with a smile on their face because they felt so passionate about their work? This would be a wonderful thing for both children and adults to learn how to do. And all of that can be taught through Montessori education.

Entertainment: Feeding Your Brain the Good Stuff

What we feed our bodies has a big effect on our physical health. So what we feed our brains have a big influence on our mental health. Americans consume a lot of entertainment that often does horrible damage to their mental state. Until just a few weeks ago I was guilty of this. I watched a lot of political videos on YouTube because I needed something to watch and didn't have many shows that I knew about that actually interested me. And these videos really did lower my happiness. But then one political video upset me so much that I had insomnia that night and it threw me off the whole week. I finally realized that I needed to make a change. So I started thinking back to when I can remember TV being enjoyable. It really hasn't been since I was a kid. And so I decided to start watching shows I enjoyed as a kid when life was simpler.

Right now I'm restricting the stuff I watch to "Mr. Roger's Neighborhood, "Between the Lions," interviews with Mr. Rogers, and some Jews for Jesus stuff. Different things work for different people. I think "Mr. Roger's Neighborhood" is nice to watch because he was such a great guy and the show is so calming. "Between the Lions" is fun too because it has lots of singing and funny sketches. I already feel better by freeing myself from the political stuff. But I realized my work in this area was not done yet.

About a week ago I deleted my Facebook app. I still have the Messenger app so I can message friends and I didn't delete my Facebook account but it has still made a huge difference. For so long I would go on my phone, open the Facebook app, and start scrolling without even realizing what I was doing. Because of this, I wasn't able to cut back because how am I supposed to do that if I don't even realize I'm doing it? So many people have this problem. They go on Facebook, or some other type of social media, just wanting to scroll through things for a few minutes and end up hooked on for hours. And that would be fine if it was enjoyable. But most of it is completely mindless and some of it is pretty upsetting. I wasn't sure if I could handle deleting it because then what would I do with my free time? But now I am using my free time much more wisely to watch something relaxing or informative like I'm now watching or even to just spend more time listening to music. It really has increased my happiness. It's a scary step but it can increase your happiness too.

Food: Feeding Your Body the Good Stuff

I'm sure you've heard plenty of advice on how you have to eat healthily. I'm sure you've tried many times (assuming you're an American) because we are all so obsessed with dieting. And yet 42% of Americans are obese. At the time of writing this book, I'm one of them but I do believe it won't be for too much longer. Exercising can be an issue for many people but I've loved it for years. The issue for me had been food. I tried so hard to increase my willpower. It always failed. But then I realized what I needed to change to really make the change towards healthy eating: my mindset.

From a young age we're taught that unhealthy food is something we should want and healthy food is something we just have to deal with. Most kids are forced to eat their vegetables and get rewarded with ice cream. It was the simple way to do things because kids usually prefer junk food. But it really affects our mindset. When we think about celebrating something our mind is used to thinking that unhealthy food would be good for that. When we feel upset and need comfort food our mind is used to thinking that unhealthy food is good for that. It can be very hard to break a habit that we've been doing since before we can remember. I don't like the throw the term addiction around but honestly, the learned behavior with how we think about unhealthy food does act very much as an addiction would.

Now of course our taste buds are geared toward sugar, salt, and fat. Carbs are fun too. You see, back when we were cave people we had to work very hard to find fruit to gather and animals to kill for meat so we needed it all to be a big craving so we'd be willing to put in the effort. Vegetables on the other hand were easy to find so we didn't need to crave them. And the genes of people with these types of taste buds were more likely to get passed down because these people were more likely to have enough nutrients to survive. But the world we live in now is very difficult to manage for people with these types of taste buds. Not only are sugar, salt, and fat easy to find and very cheap but food companies have made foods much higher in addictive substances in order to get us to keep eating them. And with our busy lives, it's very tempting to get frozen meals or fast food because it'll save us the effort even if it's not as good as a home-cooked meal. It can be tough to find the energy.

For a long time, I tried the willpower thing which is what most people try. I tried denying myself the foods I wanted which just made me feel deprived and it would not last long. I'd be back to eating unhealthy food very quickly. Over time I did make some progress with healthy eating by learning how to cook simple dishes that tasted good. I enjoy salmon, eggs, and shrimp. But even though I knew the meals were yummy I still would only have 1 or 2 healthy home-cooked meals a week. And at work, I tried bringing in protein shakes but I ended up still getting hot dogs and fries. But then I came up with a new strategy. Instead of just focusing on the taste of the food I would focus on enjoying the nutrition.

You see, when we eat it often just takes a few minutes. So the joy you get from the taste of food only lasts a few minutes. After realizing this I tried looking up nutrition facts about the food I was eating and how those nutrients help the body. It actually worked very well at getting me to eat healthily and brought me a greater amount of time and joy. And as I continued to learn more about nutrition I started to take pride in healthy eating. It just would leave me with a wholesome feeling while junk food was beginning to give me an empty feeling. It takes time and I'm not out of the obese category yet but I do hope that seeing the issue of unhealthy eating as something you need to change your mindset for rather than just needing willpower will allow you to eat healthier and thus have a healthier body.

You're Never Going to Have a Perfect Life: Why That's Ok

As I've stated before, I am continuing to learn more about happiness as I am writing this book. Right now I'm about finished dealing with a cold. I don't get sick often (thank God) so I was feeling a bit sorry for myself at first. I was very upset about missing work the most. Also feeling sick isn't fun either. But yesterday I realized that God must've been trying to teach me something by making my life not status quo because I have perfected my status quo. Cutting out political videos and Facebook really finished the job. And the fact is that when life is going great we rarely learn about life. It's during the difficult periods that we learn. In fact, the whole reason I quit politics and social media was that it was upsetting me so much it gave me insomnia and messed up things for a week. I actually didn't realize that I had to improve on my status quo because I had gotten lazy about finding alternatives to politics and social media. But having that difficult experience allowed me to see the error in my ways. And I'm sure there are still ways I could potentially be happier but God has to teach me and he needs me to struggle at least a bit in order to get the message across.

I realized that I was a little angry with God at first when I got sick. I don't want you to get the wrong impression that I have a perfect relationship with God or that I appreciate everything he's given me nearly as much as I should. I don't believe anyone has a perfect relationship with God. So many of us who are given good lives fall into the trap of becoming spoiled. But I am working on it and will continuously work on it for the rest of my days. But I did find myself thinking "I've achieved perfection in the status quo version of my life. When things are going as usual I'm always having awesome days and am taking very good care of my physical health. So what could possibly be the point of God making me get sick and have some difficult days?" Well, it made me think of how others could misinterpret what I had meant by happiness capitalism. Once in an English class, the whole class was complaining about how my teacher was too harsh of a grader. One girl said the class was stressing her out. I thought that was a weird complaint because school is work and working well at times stresses you out. Yes, I do still think Montessori would be a better school model but even then learning can still be stressful. And life is but a series of classes taught by God that are oftentimes incredibly difficult and I've for sure had plenty of Fs. But that's ok because nobody's life is perfect. Life isn't meant to be that way. And that's just something we have to accept.

What started getting me to think about this today was watching a Youtube video called "Where's Your Joy?" The pastor (Steven Furtick) was talking about how the bible doesn't say that we should just search for or pray for joy. Doing so will likely make us more miserable because constantly evaluating our lives for happiness is not a helpful thing to do. But the way the bible says to achieve joy is to make the difficult things in our lives the good things in our lives. I realized that this means I should not see these difficult days as God being mean to me for no reason but to see them as learning days. I kind of already knew that but it helps to have reminders. Seriously if you do try to put the lessons from this book into your lives PLEASE do not expect it to work on the first try. It takes a lot of life "classes" to truly learn just one lesson. And of course, as always, this has to do with not just memorizing a lesson but changing your mindset. As you start implementing lessons into your life you can remember the successes you've had with learning and that will make future learning come much easier for you.

I know it's tempting to want a perfect life. I mean who wouldn't wish for a life that was fun all of the time? But the thing that I've noticed during my own experience is that when life gets too close to perfect I take it for granted. A few months ago 74% of my days were awesome days. (I'm insanely spoiled). It was amazing but I didn't appreciate it. I was upset with God for not making it at least 90% of my days. I had become very entitled. So of course that percentage went down in the next 2 months but it was still the majority of my days. And I didn't appreciate that. Now that I've had a few difficult days I think I'm putting things more in perspective. It's helping me not be the type of entitled person that I can't stand. And maybe someday I'll be able to have a ton and really appreciate it. But in the meantime, I have to learn all I can on my difficult days. And doing so will more than pay off. It's not perfect but perfect can be overrated.

Is Pursuing Happiness a Selfish Thing?

One of the big complaints many people have about people who are trying to achieve happiness is that it is a selfish goal. Many people assume that if you're working on yourself you're not thinking about others. But this could not be farther from the truth. Yes, when you begin your happiness journey you may be focused on your own goals but if you manage to achieve your goal of having happiness then you'll naturally want to spread it.

You may be thinking right now of people out there who get their happiness from putting others down. It seems like there are many people out there like that. But in reality, those types of people are really just miserable to an extreme. The reason why they put others down is that they feel terrible about themselves. There was one study that found that bullies are even more depressed than the people they bully. Why? Because they're so full of misery that they can't help but spread it. We all spread what we have whether we're trying to or not. Think back to a time when you were in a bad mood. You may have taken it out on a family member, friend, or stranger because you just felt so terrible and you thought you'd feel better if you let it out. But afterward, you most likely felt an empty feeling and were angry at yourself. Bad people feel this too. The difference is they convince themselves that the other person was horrible and deserved it. This makes them feel a little better at the moment but over time they become more and more hateful and take out their self-loathing on others because they don't want to admit that they now hate themselves.

But what about happy people? Happy people are able to move past the basic emotions of anger and jealousy and are able to take pride in being kind and making others happy. It's an amazingly good feeling to know you made someone's day a little better. And being the type of person that makes other people happy will make you even happier as long as you're genuine about it. It's a beautiful process that truly makes the life of happy people wonderful as well.

Being happy can also lead to you making a positive difference in the world and will lower your chance of making a negative difference. So many people who are unhappy watch the news religiously in order to distract from their own lives. But this only makes them more miserable. You see, people usually only watch news channels that already agree with their point of view. So their views on things don't really change but they can become more extremist. Then they will make the world worse by demonizing those on the other end of the political spectrum or even people who are just moderate in their opinions. Miserable people often think that the world is a horrible place and it needs to be burned down because whatever rises from the ashes would be better than what we have now. Given, there are a lot of problems in the world. But trying to fix them through hate is not going to go well.

I'd like you now to try to picture what the world would be like if it was filled with happy people. People would definitely be much nicer to one another. They wouldn't be taking out their misery on others because they wouldn't be miserable in the first place. People would be far less likely to smoke or eat a ton of junk food because they wouldn't have to distract themselves from their overwhelming feelings. This would lead to people living longer and being less sick while still alive. People would also volunteer more and give more to charity because not only would they be less territorial with their money but they would know that the people they were giving to were good-hearted hardworking people who would not take advantage of the kindness they received. So many of our world's problems would be solved just like that. And if people disagreed on how to solve a certain issue they would be able to sit down with each other and calmly discuss their points of view like adults are supposed to. It would be a wonderful world that would just keep getting better and better.

What I would also like you to know is that you deserve to be happy. Yes, you will most likely have to work hard to achieve it but if you do become happier it's nothing to feel guilty about. Even if you've messed up and have been mean to others I do still believe you deserve happiness. If you are in that type of situation and believe in God I would suggest the song "Forgivable" by MercyMe. It goes over that no matter how much you've messed up in life you still are deserving of God's love. And even if you don't believe in God you still do deserve to feel happiness. Getting down on yourself and keeping yourself from achieving true happiness is not helping anyone. It will likely make you mess up even more. But if you realize that you are worthy of love and happiness it will not only help you but also make the world a better place.

God's Love is For Everyone: And Yes I Do Mean Everyone

Before deciding to write this chapter I really didn't want to write a chapter specifically about God. Yes, I've mentioned God quite a bit in this book but for some reason, I thought a chapter specifically dedicated to him would be too much. I also thought people would get a bad feeling from me telling them that God loves them because it's such a common phrase among charlatans. I'm not trying to get anyone to feel good just so they'll donate to my charity that I'm obviously stealing money from. I'm also not trying to convert anybody. I'm not a missionary and as a Jew, I'm really not a fan of people who are there to push their Christian beliefs on others. (The people who encouraged me to become a Christian didn't force it on me at all.) If the subject makes you feel uncomfortable it's fine to skip this chapter. I believe there's only one more chapter after this I'm going to write. But if you do believe in God or even if you don't but want to hear what I have to say I would recommend you read this part.

Now it is true that many people who preach about God often make people feel like they're unloved by God. This could be about people who've made mistakes or even people who haven't done anything wrong but believe that just who they are is a sinner because of others' interpretations of God's rules. I'm well aware of the fact that many people who preach the gospel scare a lot of people into thinking that they're going to hell or that God hates them. The fact is there are many people out there who have hearts so full of hate that rather than questioning their beliefs assume that God must be hateful too. It can be difficult not to take what these people say as hurtful.

Of course, many people, which at one time included me, feel that God either doesn't exist or is just a very hateful ruler because they've dealt with many difficult circumstances and felt that God either abandoned them or purposefully made them suffer because he hates them. Now I'm not trying to interpret the reasons for other people's suffering because I just can't know but I can tell you about my experiences with God. You see when my depression began I tried to have a closer relationship with God. I started praying a lot and going to the temple every Saturday. I was even partially kosher. But it just really didn't seem to help. This led me to become agnostic because it was too painful for me to believe in God when I was certain he hated me. Over the next couple of years, I kept going back and forth between believing in God and not believing. Then my junior year of college I joined a Christian group and was so impressed with how much joy believing in God and Jesus brought to the people in the group. It made me feel like maybe I could be joyous in my belief. But after college things began going really horribly for me so I once again believed that God hated me and once again dealt with that by believing God wasn't real.

Now, as I explained earlier in this book, I did eventually get better. I also found a great church. I did believe in God at this point but in the back of my mind, I still felt that he may hate me. It took well over a year for me to see things differently. I slowly realized that I would have never become as happy as I am today if I hadn't been through those years of suffering. Now, this is not to say that it was my fault or that mental illness is a good thing. I am definitely not signing up for going through those hard times again. But I feel that going through those times gave me the choice to now be miserable about the unfairness of it or happy that I survived it and learned from it. I chose the latter and was grateful for being given this choice. This is not to say that I'm any better than those who still struggle to deal with horrible things that happened to them in the past. I'm a very blessed person and not everyone has the privileges that I have. It's not about having a feeling of superiority but just doing what worked best for me.

It is so hard to believe that God loves you when you've been suffering for so long and are continuing to suffer. I'm not saying that praying or improving your relationship with God will cure your problems. It'd be nice if it was that simple but it isn't so. I'm not going to quote bible verses about God's love because I believe that's more of an intellectual argument and I realize that you need more of a focus on the emotional part of it. I don't think a bible quote or religious saying is going to lessen the pain of your suffering if you don't believe God's looking out for you. I don't hold the secret to being able to understand God's plans. I think I understand at least some of his plans with me but even then I have a good chance of being wrong. I would just like to leave you with the thought that maybe just maybe you'll change your mind about whether or not God loves you too if you start seeing meaning in your suffering.

Happiness is NOT a Right

I'm sure you're anxious to get to the last chapter of the book already but as I said before I'm writing this book in real-time so I keep coming up with more ideas for more chapters. In this chapter, I would like to share my experience of being really spoiled and not appreciating God until yesterday. I was sick this last week and a half and what you need to understand is that I find it very helpful when things aren't going my way to look at it as an act of God that's pointing me in the right direction because I've gone astray. This may not work for everyone but it has been very helpful for me.

Anyway, I am writing this chapter on January 16, 2023. So far the year has not been nearly as happy as 2022 had been. Yes, it is ridiculous that I'm judging the year off of 16 days. This chapter is about me being ridiculous. Anyway, I have to admit that I was getting a little angry with God up until yesterday. Only a third of my days this month as of yesterday had been awesome. This was a big decrease for me because in the last 4 months of 2022 over half of my days, each month were awesome. But then last night I read a magazine article that my dad had gotten me about happiness. One section of the article talked about how "the pursuit of happiness" is guaranteed to us Americans in the Constitution. And then it hit me. We are guaranteed the pursuit of happiness, not happiness itself.

You see I've been unbelievably blessed, especially in 2022 so I had become really spoiled. I thought that I had the right to awesome days and I was angry at God for decreasing mine. But God never guaranteed me any awesome days. He hasn't promised that to anyone. But I was looking at each awesome day as no big deal because it was just my right and any day that was less than awesome was God cheating me. Luckily I've changed my mindset to see awesome days as a blessing and other types of days as fine. I can't guarantee I won't get spoiled again but for now, I think I'm good. And ironically today ended up being an awesome day. And I thank God for that.

Now, most people have not been given as much as I have in terms of awesome days but still, plenty of people do believe that happiness is a right. We are often taught that if someone disagrees with our opinion of the world and that makes us unhappy it's their fault that we are unhappy. But at the end of the day, happiness really does begin, continue, and end with gratitude. I can't say enough about gratitude which I'm sure is getting annoying. But it is true. If you're going to be happy you need to take ownership of your happiness and not focus on blaming God or other people for cheating you out of the happiness that you think you have the right to. And ironically this will make you happier.

Happiness is a Choice Kind of

I really don't like it when people say the very much overused line "happiness is a choice." It is partially true. I hope this book will help you make the right choices for achieving happiness. But it's not going to happen overnight by any means. You see, when people say "happiness is a choice" it implies that if you're unhappy it's because you're choosing to be. Yes, there are people who enjoy being miserable but at least 95% of people want to be happy (I assume). And you can make your brain more prone to happiness by choosing good things to do for it. But it's not going to be as simple as being miserable and then just deciding to be happy and boom you're happy. You can change your brain but it's going to take quite a bit of time.

If you've researched the psychology of happiness you may have heard that happiness is around 50% genetic. First of all, that is such bullshit. In order to calculate that you'd have to be able to quantify happiness. How can you quantify happiness? You can ask people to rate their happiness on a scale of 1 to 10 but different people and different cultures define happiness in different ways so how would that be accurate? Some cultures discourage happiness a lot so people living in that area of the world who are happy will hide it so as not to offend others. And some cultures think happiness is the most important thing ever so people living in those areas will try desperately to seem happy even if they're dying inside. I do believe there is some genetic component to happiness because some people are born happier than others. But even if you are born happy there are plenty of ways to make yourself miserable just like if you're born miserable there are plenty of ways to make yourself happy. Before I was 25 I was never really a happy person. Even before the bipolar kicked in. But over the last 3 years, thanks to good choices, I have become extremely happy. So don't let psychologists who preach the genetic component as an end all be all of the happiness get you down.

The reason why I'm including this chapter (besides wanting to rant) is that I want to provide some further instructions about how to use this book for your benefit. I would strongly suggest not trying to implement all of the tips in this book at once. It takes time to change your beliefs. Even if you now believe something in this book that I've advised, that doesn't mean your brain believes it. You need to give your brain time to change by practicing thinking in a new way. If you've been training your brain to be unhappy for years it's going to take a considerable amount of time to make it prone to happiness. But that doesn't mean it will never happen.

The last thing I would like to make very clear is to NOT use this book as a way to judge others. I just know someone will though. Some people just love an excuse to look down on others. And some people may try to help others using this book but may have gotten the wrong message from it. I am BEGGING you not to use this book as an excuse to tell someone who just got diagnosed with cancer to just "look on the bright side." I believe that the 5 biggest issues a person can face are: absolute poverty, physical illness, mental illness, trauma, and loss. I've had more struggles than most with mental illness but luckily for me, I've never experienced any of the other 4. I don't know how to overcome the other ones. I will fully admit that. I'm not saying it's impossible for people with these issues to overcome their challenges but I'm not going to be the one to give advice on those subjects. Please use this book to strengthen yourself and not to put others down. I just know there will be people who ignore that plea but I hope the majority will not.

The Final Chapter: Thank You so, so Much

Congratulations! You've made it to the end! What I'm about to say may seem like I'm just sucking up to you so you'll write a good review on Amazon but trust me when I say that I actually mean it. I am so grateful to you for giving me the opportunity to help you at least a little. This book may have been a waste of time for you and if so I apologize for that. But if this book taught you at least one useful tip for achieving happiness I would call that a success for me! So many people think that helping others is easy and that if they just put in the minimal effort they'll change people's lives. This is of course not true at all. It is so difficult to just find the opportunity to help others to say nothing of actually succeeding in helping others.

A few months ago I got hired at a clinic as a Recovery Support Specialist and I absolutely love it. Not only am I helping people but it allowed me to go from being very happy to be extremely happy. It's greedy of me to want more but if I did help you I am very grateful. If I can get one person who reads this book to have one awesome day because of it I consider that a success! You see, I suffered from mental illness for a long time and was always in the position of being the one who badly needed help. I could only dream of being in a position where I was doing well and I could actually help others who needed help. But thanks to many wonderful people I did get better. And thanks to the people who hired me I now have the opportunity to help others I always dreamed of. And if I helped you thank you for helping me fulfill even more of my dream. Hopefully, this book will allow you to become happier and perhaps one day feel the joy of helping others successfully too. Once again, thank you!

Made in United States
North Haven, CT
24 April 2023

35814343R00065